DAVID PEARSON

THE CHURCH...TO ROCK STONE

Reflecting on the Jamaican Church for National Transformation

EMI
Extra MILE Innovators
Kingston, Jamaica WI

COPYRIGHT

Unless otherwise noted, all scripture references are taken from *The New Living Translation*, Copyright © 1996, Tyndale House Foundation

Published by
Extra MILE Innovators
54 Montgomery Avenue,
Kingston 10, Jamaica W.I.
www.extramileja.com
ruthtaylor@extramileja.com
Tele: (1876) 782-9893

Cover, Layout, and eBook by
N.D. Author Services [NDAS]
www.NDAuthorServices.com

DEDICATION

To, Cynthia, my wonderful wife of 25 years; your encouragement has been constant and your support vital. I still believe that marrying you has been the best thing I have ever done in my life, outside of my decision to accept Christ.

ENDORSEMENT

Absolutely delightful! This book is a mixed bag of deep common-sense philosophical reflections on society, as well as a loving and probing critique of the contemporary church. The language is geared for most, conveying a conviction that in turn 'imposes' conviction on the reader, as the author writes with passion concerning truth and justice. The book is prophetic.

—Dr. Delano V. Palmer,
Former Deputy President,
Jamaica Theological Seminary

ACKNOWLEDGMENTS

I wish to say a special thanks to Rev. Dr. Garnett Roper, who has had the most significant impact on my theological thought throughout the years, and who has constantly encouraged me to write. Through you, Rev., the Bible has become truly meaningful—hopefully, I can make it meaningful to others.

Thanks also to Dr. Delano Palmer, who has always amazed me with his ability to find humour in every situation. Sometimes I really want to be like him, but that would be a bigger joke than the jokes I could conjure up. Still, his wit and humour surely lift the gloom that engulfs sombre writers. He too has constantly encouraged me to write.

FOREWORD

I first met David Pearson when he was a student in my Greek Grammar class in the early 1980s at the Jamaica Theological Seminary. I was foolish enough to dare any student to get an A in my class as it was impossible. David got an A. His erudition ought therefore never again to surprise me. And yet again he has in this work.

This work is refreshing because of its erudition, curiosity, breadth and depth of reflection and its courage. I was particularly stunned and flattered when I found in these pages, an essay, which was a succinct summary of an impromptu address I had given in a JTS staff meeting. All staff meetings that are held biweekly include a fairly long diatribe by me as President that is a cross between a state of the church presentation and a devotional exercise. What surprised me was the diligence of the treatment and how David had made my argument as if they were his own seem so cogent. It may be a little thing but it tells you everything about David. He is forever the researcher and student, always contemplative and reflective, and like a beaver, he stores things for future consumption.

David is a theologian who has emerged from among the Christian Brethren movement in Jamaican. He is every bit a product of that Movement, by his love of family, diligent interest in the Scriptures, his love of young people and his evangelistic fervour. Those of us who have paid attention to the Christian Brethren movement would have thought its dispensational reading strategy, its pro-Israel politics (some would say its right wing ideology) and recalcitrant patriarchy ought to have been fatal flaws in this young theologian. Yet there is none of that turgid starchiness in this work. The range of subject covered, the questions included, the openness of dialogue belie David's denominational upbringing.

There is warmth of love and friendship and the joy of family percolating through this work. Everything is here from the parity, reciprocity and mutuality in all matters with his wife, to getting his adolescent boys to do their domestic chores, with their father very much leading by example. Also in these pages is his struggle to deal with the pilgrimage of his friend Ric Couchman who is no longer confessing the faith that David and himself held. I would have liked for David to have been a tad bit kinder in his treatment of my friend Omar Davies, with whose lecture delivered at JTS David also interacted. For that manner he was not particularly kind also to the JLP leader and present Prime Minister Andrew Holness. His treatment of these two is at worse testament to the rigorous honesty of the work.

"The Church to Rock Stone" is nicely organized. It is 12 essays (or perhaps more accurate 15 pieces, since there are three poems composed by David among the chapters at the start of each section). The chapters are organized in three sections each of which ends with questions for the reader to engage and discuss. The first section bears the title "A Cock-Eyed Vision of the Gospel?" It is the public theology flavour in the work as it seeks to interact with matters of context and the issue of relevance.

The second section deals with the Church in Community: this is the most theologically self-conscious section of the book. It is a thoroughgoing critique without appearing to set out to do so of the modern practice of Christianity among the section of the church to which David belongs. He argues for example that the church's inadequate involvement in community is perhaps because its leadership does not know how to engage with the community. His critique is gentle and disarming, free of bombast and self-righteousness. It is criticism from within and it is of a fellow pilgrim searching for a praxis that is redeeming in response to the lived reality of the people.

Third section is about Caring Again. Here David is seen both as a father and as a son with aged parents. It is practical theology. Forever, the eclectic theologian, researcher and thinker is just a human being. He brings his faith into his home, like Jesus in the home of Mary and Martha, though he does not himself reference them, concerned with domestic duties.

This work is a welcome addition to the body of literature called Caribbean Theology. It has achieved that because it is doing theology rather than reading theology. It is engaged with matters of context, it is theology in fragments, it is questions, it is the work of a different interlocutor. However, in his case the chasm between the Seminary and the church and the church and the community and the community and the family have been bridged. It is a must read for beginning theology students and pastors and everyone else in between.

—Rev. Dr. Garnett Roper, President,
Jamaica Theological Seminary

TABLE OF CONTENTS

ROCK STONE

The man heard my name
And pondered its meaning.
Was it an outburst of surprise,
Of perplexity exclaiming?
Or did it speak of my hide,
As hard as a rhinoceros's horn,
Or as tough as a well walked path,
My unfeeling nature shown?
Maybe the nature of my brain
And the futility of learning is in view;
Whatever it is he opined that
Negative connotations only grew.
Another suggested with a warning
That the name might speak
Of the weapons used by David
To show the giant weak.
"Better hold your tongue
And consider the best;
Instead of ridiculing a stranger
Why not live at peace and rest?"
They both looked at me
Waiting for some elaboration,
But I immediately walked away
With nary an explanation.

What's in a name? My Facebook name, Rock Stone, has a particular history behind it that reminds me of a momentous decision I made concerning my outlook on life. In July 2013, as my wife and I celebrated our 20th wedding anniversary at a hotel on Jamaica's North Coast, I threatened to spoil our time together, having been in a sombre mood from a series of Facebook interactions that simply boggled my mind. I had offered my thoughts on a particularly controversial topic on a friend's page, and the raging debate that had been going on long before I joined suddenly focussed on me, with vitriol poured out because I had "bashed some persons with the Bible." The truth is that I had taken no side in the argument, or so I thought, but had instead come down on a middle path asking participants to try to be sympathetic to the difficulties each discussed person faced, in spite of whatever stance he took. Additionally, I did not quote or make reference to the Bible, nor even identify myself as a Christian. These things left me confused since I neither knew any of those who came against me nor had interacted with them before. They were Facebook friends of one of my Facebook friends.

After that incident, one of the persons who had attacked me begun to show-up in various discussions with many of my friends, and continued his sustained attacks against me. I just could not understand this, since I hardly ever quote the Bible, nor do I speak of my faith in ways that do not promote the well-being of those on the margins of society, even if they are not Christians. As the attacks became more and more personal I became more and more sombre. At that anniversary vacation, my wife, Cynthia, encouraged me to take action instead of sitting back in pained silence. There, in Ocho Rios, it suddenly occurred to me that this offensive individual had been reading my Facebook profile and forming conclusions because I was a theologian at what is considered to be a conservative seminary in Jamaica. Apparently, in his world, he had formed conclusions about persons like me, and since they typically are forceful in their opinions against him he assumed that I was like them (or so it seemed). He was openly antagonistic to people of faith, and literally trolled Facebook to bash those who did not share his "brighter" position. Before realizing his modus operandi I had attempted to reason with him on a number of topics but soon found such futile. He belittled those who did not share his ideas, distorted their comments, engaged in revisionist history about anything to do with Christianity, and invited like-minded friends to "engage in his party." He then sent me a Facebook friend request, which I rejected. One day out of tremendous frustration to his constant name-calling and character assassinations I responded harshly to him, something I do not do normally in any sphere of life.

So, Cynthia and I were in Ocho Rios celebrating our anniversary. The beautiful scenery of the coastal hillside location that overlooked the turquoise waters of the Caribbean Sea and the wonderful resort accommodations were lost on me due to my sour mood. Worse, my wonderful wife of twenty years, who expected a bit more attention from her husband on this special occasion, was not very pleased with my distracted demeanour. So we sat down and spoke about it, and she convinced me to take action. I removed myself from every group in which that individual showed up, and turned off notifications to them. I also decided that less personal information about me was the wise way to go since this individual had demonstrated that lunatics do profile persons based on information they can garner about them. As such, I purged my personal information and decided to change my name. You see, I could have decided to withdraw from social media altogether, but I had linked-up with long lost friends who resided in different parts of the world, and I do enjoy communicating with them. Facebook was a place where I shared my new found interest in poetry as well as some occasional thoughts on matters related to the relevance of my faith. A name change could buy me some time, I thought, as along with the other steps I had taken this individual would find it difficult to track me down (it took him about a month). But what should that change be?

I recall sitting on the bed with Cynthia beside me as we spoke about the possible name change. "What name are you going to use?" My response came fairly quickly, but it was not out of a sense of conviction about the name I uttered. I merely uttered the name to say that any name would do. "I don't know, maybe Rock Stone!" Cynthia laughed at the suggestion, not a laughter of derision but one which asked, "Where did such a choice come from?" You see, the term "rock stone" in Jamaica is often a colloquial expression with various possible meanings; it might be a sort of stand-alone, swear term of incredulity ("Rock stone!"), or it may be used various ways adjectivally: it describes the huge extent of an action ("He got a rock stone beating!"), or the dedication to a task or political party ("He's a rock stone Labourite," i.e. an ardent and lifelong supporter of the Jamaica Labour Party), or even a person's daftness ("His head is as tough as rock stone."). I can see why Cynthia laughed at my suggestion, but in the next moment I liked the name and went and changed it instantly. Since that day I have been Rock Stone of Facebook.

The change of name brought with it a certain sense of freedom to "start over," so to speak. I became bolder in the sharing of my ideas, though I am still committed to a non-confrontational stance, and I have become more vocal about matters of my faith, especially the ideas I see being corrupted by a Church that often loses its way by following popular trends to make Christians feel good. We live in a world where Biblical ideas are unpopular, and the life of faith is perceived as being more and more irrelevant to today's reality. I am particularly challenged by a strident anti-intellectualism and irrationality (inside and outside the Church) that parades itself as faith and makes a mockery of the Biblical principles upon which Christians have lived for centuries.

We live in a world that is currently engulfed in "post-factualism," which creates new realities based on slight and suggestion, and what we can get people to believe, whether or not it is true. We may decide to go with the flow and touch people where their felt needs and egos can be stroked, but the doctor who does that with a cancer patient while withholding the truth of the diagnosis can be guaranteed that her treatment of the patient will not treat the problem. Inside that patient's body, the sickness is strengthening and spreading with dastardly consequences. The same is true in a world and a Church that hides from the truth. We must speak the truth as we find ways of engaging those who have imbibed the popular philosophies of the day only to see that their lives and daily experiences leave them empty. That is what I attempt to do in this little book; I also hope that I do it with clarity and love.

My primary interest is that Christians will take matters related to all aspects of their lives and view them through the lens of Scripture. If we do not engage the world in meaningful ways we will find ourselves navel-gazing, and spouting ideas that only warm the air around our mouths. And for too long that has been the way we have operated. So this is my reflection of the Church as it faces today's reality, especially in Jamaica. These are only contextual reflections, though I believe that many lessons are prevalent in them that are applicable to the Church anywhere. But they are not meant to be the final word on any of the issues, though I do hope that they will provide us with a platform to sure up our faith in a dying world. These are but my ideas about the Church in Jamaica today, hence my title, "The Church...to Rock Stone."

Coram Deo
Signal Hill, Tobago
March 2018

Introduction:
I am a Theologian

One of the common strategies for coming to some understanding of the people we meet is to ask them about their profession. You know, "Nice meeting you, Junior. What do you do for a living?" Our attitude to the person is often affected by their response. I once met a young lady who, in response to my query, informed me that she worked with a law firm. She seemed so unassuming that my bias shone through easily: "Are you a legal secretary?" Her slightly annoyed response made me wish that the ground would open and swallow me up. "I am a lawyer and partner in the firm." My attitude towards her was never the same again. I suspect that if she had confirmed my bias I would have thought of her differently. Since that experience, I have tried not to repeat that bias. But now, when someone asks me that question, I proudly declare my profession with a little smirk as I anticipate their responses: "I am a Theologian." Silence... gratuitous comment... small talk... change the subject.

One lady responded to my declaration after the obligatory pause: "That's great... We need more people to think of the religious aspects of life. ..Where do your children go to school?" Another time a man (I was at a party at his house) who admittedly has never been involved in church, said when he heard of my profession, that he himself did not see how the Sabbath could be Sunday. He reminded his wife not to serve me alcohol since I was a "man of the cloth," and then proceeded, "Oh, haven't we been having some great weather of late?" Temptations to comment that God had been giving us some good weather as a part of his gracious benevolence, awaiting our repentance, were steadfastly rebuffed on my part; but only just.

No one has asked the pragmatic question that my mother did when I told her I was going to study theology. I suspect that many people have the same question but are afraid to ask. Of course, my mother would not be afraid: "How much money can you make from that?" I had no answer to that question and was quite frustrated that I had not considered it. What did this say about my own concern for my future family? After all, was I not brought up to believe that a man should ensure that he chooses a profession to care for his family? What was I signing up for? I had no answers.

Maybe the most interesting question I have been asked about my profession came from a friend who himself had been considering life's ultimate concerns. He is a famous Jamaican artist and has turned his back on the traditional teachings of the church he grew up in with his four siblings, led by his father, the founding Bishop. My friend Philip asked, "As a theologian what do you tell people to believe, in terms of church doctrine?" On reflection, this is exactly what many church people believe that theologians ought to do, and is the basis for their greatest concerns—"Do you teach people about eternal security?" "What do you teach about the rapture?" "Do you teach that the scriptures are inerrant?" "How do you explain Joshua's long day?" "Was Jesus fully man or fully God?" "Should all Christians speak in tongues...be baptized in the name of Jesus or the Trinity...be immersed or sprinkled... can Christians masturbate?"

My older son has borne the brunt of his father's "dubious" profession. He was not been allowed to enjoy a normal, teenaged development, at least as he began those tumultuous years. At one family function his cousins constantly taunted him about his need to avoid various "ungodly" practices—"Bwoy, don't drink no beer and mine how yu a talk to the girl; word might a get back to yu father!" After all, theologians are these goofy persons who specialize in living life in a manner contrary to normal development and go about the place like cosmic killjoys, sucking out all the pleasures of life. To borrow a line from James Baldwin, when theologians make love to their spouses, it is "joyless rockings." According to this philosophy, my boys will need to quickly understand that laughter is the garment of the shallow since the Lord loves those who gravely reflect on life and walk around with a sombre face from those musings.

If we think of it, being a theologian in Jamaica today is not as fashionable or important as many other professions. Take for instance that of being a Pollster. Pollsters often hold our country at rapt attention, especially when we face a general election. Political parties and media houses pay these voting prognosticators huge sums of money for them to unfurl their eagerly anticip- ated findings at strategically important times. I suspect that these men are paid handsomely for each poll they conduct, and each time one result is published there comes the promise of another in a few weeks. Usually, just before elections there are at least three polls making predictions on a constituency by constituency basis. What's so interesting is that the polls often have differ- ent findings; in other words, at least two are usually wrong. But this does not stop pollsters from collecting their "long bags." Polling is profitable even if your findings are dubious, at least in Jamaica today. And since you make a lot of money from it, the absurdity of your findings really does not impact on onlookers significantly. It stands to reason then, that being a pollster is much more desirable than being a theologian.

Another profession that puts people in good stead in today's Jamaica is that of an Economist. Political parties and government technocrats draw heavily on the knowledge and expertise of some of the best minds in the discipline locally. Today's economists speak a very distinct language as they recommend macro-solutions for the macro-problems, causing fiscal woes to macro-numbers of our population. Of course, they differ on just how these macro-level problems will be solved. Some economists speak of aligning macro-variables that will lead to stability and job creation by the private sector, hence creating prosperity for the masses. Others speak of government intervention to kick-start the economy for the creation of those jobs. Yet, despite much column inches and air-time devoted to the matter, people are still experiencing macro-suffering as we try to make our micro-salaries stretch past its first day in our hands. Perhaps there is something to the fancy

sounding macro terms that makes these economists popular. Theologians perhaps need to
understand that the use of expansive language
will gain us a better hearing. Maybe next time I
will address the church and nation about the
macro-level missing of God's mark by our
people which transpires into mega-difficulties
for all and sundry, impacting on our abilities to
enjoy life even at the micro level. I speak the
truth—more often than not when I hear these
economists speak I am certain that they are Mar-
tians, speaking the language of the green planet.
But who cares? They sound expensive and are
paid handsomely for their gobbledegook. (Truth-
fully, I have heard some theologians master this
art too—but they are fewer than you think).

How about Lawyers? I am told that they are a
dime a dozen in Jamaica today, and that there
are many more bad lawyers than good ones. But
a recently aired "soap-opera" in Jamaica regaled
the qualities of great lawyers; some became instant celebrities. The very best know how to use
multi-syllable words, unheard of by the average
person before. They know how to hold those
words back, just to be revealed at the right time
after seemingly endless, pedantic and inane
questions. *"Did you sign the book?" "On what
page did you sign it?" "What colour ink did you
use?" "Was it a Parker pen or a Schaffer?" "At*

precisely what time did you sign?" "Did you say it was a Schaffer or Parker pen?" "Did you sign on the line, above the line or under the line?" "Sir, let me declare to you that you are PATHO-LOGICALLY MENDACIOUS!" After many hours of some of the most senseless banter on all sides, that particular soap opera provided no sensible ending, unless you are a good lawyer of course, and collected your macro-millions of dollars. This certainly leads to the floccinaucinihilipili-fication of common-sense, but who cares? This is certainly one act a theologian could not pull off and so he is not deserving of any pay.

But what about the ubiquitous profession of being a Politician? The Politician's job descrip-tion requires him to turn up for work once every four or five years and to make as much of a monkey of himself as he can. He is required to make the most outlandish comments from public platforms, deny any semblance of intelli-gence, sling tons of mud on would-be oppon-ents and detractors, point out their faults, distort their words, and lie about their doings, while at the same time shouting loudly enough in an at-tempt to hide his own short-comings. Of course, he has to be dressed in the obligatory green or orange. These men (and women) do not earn enough to own a home in short order, yet so many are so handsomely paid (from whatever sources) for their buffoonery that they can own multi-million dollar residences in a matter of a year or two. Perhaps the politicians do deserve every cent that they can put their hands on (or at least many of them) since they have to sacrifice so much of their character and intelligence to gain what they have. But theologians certainly will not get away with that, maybe because they are not ambitious enough.

I am a theologian. Notice that I did not say that "I am a preacher." Many of the finer qualities I have extolled above can be found in many preachers, but a theologian's calling is different. We are not expected to sway many people with our musings, at least that's how it seems since most of our constituents reject our "wisdom" unless it rubber stamps theirs. When we use big words we are rebuffed as being too learned for any useful purpose. If we point to the faults of others we are told that we must first remove the log from our eyes before taking the speck out of others. And do not speak of owning big houses; the theologian who miraculously achieves that is certainly a drug dealer or scammer, and most definitely is not as hardworking and honest as... say a politician. But I will continue to proudly declare my profession—I AM A THEOLOGIAN!

Being a theologian has afforded me a perspective on life that allows me to explain the behaviour above on all sides; as Bishop Fulton Sheen says, "The doctrine of original sin is the only philosophy empirically verifiable by two thousand years of human history." It also allows me the luxury of pointing out those schemes that will or will not fail, depending on the place of people's welfare in them. The theologian that I am does not furnish me with many points of discrete knowledge on esoteric matters. But it reminds me that our social space must be governed by fairness, justice, and peace for the most vulnerable and that as a people who claim to love God we must exhibit those virtues wherever we land ourselves. Maybe these things are too costly to the personal ambitions of those who are self-seeking. But the death of such virtues is the green-light for shallow economists, pollsters, lawyers, politicians, preachers and, yes, theologians to lead us astray while swelling their own coffers.

It is with the eye of a Christian theologian, who believes that the things of God must have particular relevance to the daily realities of life that I write this little book. Much of these reflections were adapted from ideas I shared on my Facebook page, where I go by the name "Rock Stone." Some were also derived from my first blog found at church2deworl.worldpress.com. I am particularly interested in Jamaicans as a people who claim a special relationship with God (almost the entire population), and for that matter, I often reflect on the Church. I do so with no ill-intent, desiring to see our churches share the transforming message of the Gospel, which brings true transformation for individuals and communities that embrace it. I share as a Christian theologian who is driven by Godly concern.

What is your profession?

PART I:
A "COCK-EYED" VISION
OF THE GOSPEL?

CONTEXTUAL PAGE RAGE

Dastardly
De-contextualized
Deliveries
Obfuscate
Truth
And adjudicate
To subjugate
The powerless
To placate
The interests
Of the powerful.
They infuriate
The prophets
Who separate
God's intention
From the pretention
Of those who
Claim to speak
As divine projection.
The Oracle exposes
Biased predilections
That confound
In ways profound,
To the extent
That the oppressed
Their own demise express

As divine intent.
Holy Writ
Lays bare
Man's lack of care
For brother
And sister
Whom he recasts
As inferior,
Of less value
Than the stature
Of the divine image
In which all are created.
Texts written
Out of oppression
Will always
Denounce repression
If read in context,
And not as a pretext
For man's dehumanizing
Selfishness.
So, up with Garvey,
Bogle and Gordon,
Bonhoeffer, King, and X,
Romero, Gutierrez;
Cone, Wright, and Francis,
Reuther, Walker, and Toussaint;
Nanny, Sharpe, Fanon,
Mandela, Tutu, and others
Angered by the

Senseless injustice
That uglies the Divine Heart.

The message of the Bible is often so different from how it is portrayed by many churches that one wonders if it is being read at all by those who most often proclaim it. The many divisions within Christendom gather around small and discrete understandings of the faith and the fervency with which those differences are defended often muddy the picture of a loving and just God who is most concerned about his creature's wellbeing. We need a renewed vision of God's people in the world; in all facets of life, we need people who understand the times and the shifts in human thinking that seek to distort and destroy the image of God in others, especially the least, for selfish purposes. But this thinking is not for the faint of heart since it often leads to loneliness as we walk the narrow path to glory, going against the herd mentality (Matthew 7:12). A "cock-eyed" vision of the Gospel is in focus, which must be rebalanced in light of the Saviour's heart.

1.

WALKING AWAY FROM "THE FAITH"

Dear brothers and sisters, if another believer is overcome by some sin, you who are godly should gently and humbly help that person back onto the right path. And be careful not to fall into the same temptation yourself. [Galatians 6:1-2]

I have also since walked away from "faith", a faith for which I continue to maintain a profound respect and that I regard as having been immensely functional for me during a certain period of my life. The "walking away" was also by choice (on account of a rather significant event while sitting under a tree on the JTS campus), in the mold of Ivan Karamazov's "refusing the ticket", with my holding a simple philosophy that life makes sense and that people make sense.

—Ric Couchman, Graduate
Jamaica Theological Seminary, 1988

My friend Ric Couchman has been the most significant "defector" from Christianity that I personally know. Ric is amongst the most brilliant and disciplined persons that I have known, easily being in the top two or three students that I have met in my academic sojourn, whether as a student or lecturer. His "walking away" made a profound impact on us who considered him our friend. We had looked to him for counsel, inspiration, and wisdom as we sought to make our faith relevant to our daily lives. Despite the pain we felt at his leaving we can only imagine that for his family the implications were so much more painful.

In the church, persons who walk away are usually not treated with the care and understanding as the scriptures themselves admonish us (Galatians 6:1-4). Instead of the "walking delicately on rice paper" approach necessary for dealing with so many who make these difficult decisions, we "drive bulldozers through a bed of roses," as we seek to show to others, apparently, that we ourselves are made of "better and sterner" stuff. After all, we are people of faith who have found "the faith." We have nothing to be ashamed of, and anyone who walks away has shown that they simply care more for the world than God. We waste no tears on such people!

Ric's "defection" struck me very differently. I knew that my friend was neither pompous nor shallow, nor did he believe that somehow his life had been unnecessarily repressed by choosing the faith and the lifestyle that came with it, even if he has come to that belief later on in life (and I do not know that he has). As we rubbed shoulders on a daily basis, and as he searched for greater relevance to the world he lived in, his studies of the Word and the scholars we read made his considerations more difficult and even painful, and his struggles became more palpably clear to those of us who knew him. A move to New York perhaps gave him the space he needed to make the painful decisions he eventually did.

Ric and I have remained friends and I have never sought to belittle his choice, perhaps because I myself have had similar struggles. I say that my struggles are similar; they are not the same. Ric has struggled with the ideas of various scholars that have made him question reality as "the faith" has painted it. I have struggled with the fact that the church reads the scriptures in a manner that is more akin to "boundary maintenance" (the protection of our denominational/confessional distinctive) and self-preservation, as we seek to be "unsullied by the world." The scriptures that we so ardently defend paint a picture of life and our responsibilities quite differently from how "the faith" does. I have therefore walked away from "the faith" as described by the church that I have been associated with, though faith continues to be an essential part of my making sense of reality. I have struggled to articulate this up until now, but since my friend has explained himself I think that I should do the same.

I have found that we are more concerned with defending "the faith" as passed on to us, whether or not it is scriptural. Take for instance the matter of our Christology. We expend much intellectual rigour defending the "true nature of Jesus" insisting that he was and is God as much as he was a man. Anyone who differs from the particular shades of meaning that we defend is often kept at arm's length, yet perhaps the most significant teaching of Christ we give little attention to—"Anyone who desires to lead must first serve (John 13)." "Do nothing out of selfish ambition or vain conceit. Rather, in humility value others above yourselves,not looking to your own interests but each of you to the interests of the others. In your relationships with one another, have the same mindset as Christ Jesus..." (Philippians 2:3-5). It seems as if we are more concerned with Jesus as God, since that makes us aligned to the most powerful being in the universe, instead of wanting to be like Jesus as a servant and to take on the station of being the least in the world.

"The faith" I have received also insists on me living in preparation for heaven, largely by being unconcerned about the happenings of the world. It is a faith that has been defined and described by a narrow and personal piety that is best described by the things that I refrain from doing: drinking, smoking, lying, adultery, sexual promiscuity and the like. When "the faith" speaks of what it is that we do we largely remain personal (pray, fast, have devotions, attend church, etc.) or in generalities (love others and remain holy).

There is little ability to relate such personal piety to the harsh realities of life. For instance, one of my students posted on her Facebook wall that beautiful passage from 2 Corinthians 5:17 —"Therefore, if anyone is in Christ, the new creation has come:The old has gone, the new is here!" I had the temerity to ask her what that meant in practical terms as it relates to hearing the "coronation" speech of our then new Prime minister, Andrew Holness, at his party's annual conference. She could not respond and instead was content to see my question dismissed by a friend of hers who stated that the passage has nothing to do with politics. No amount of trying to convince her that the passage speaks of people with a new understanding of life in its entirety, including politics, could shake her resolve. Christians must understand that God prepares them for the life of faith which looks to the next world, not the vagaries of this life and its dirty politics, she insisted. She fails to see the result—as conscientious Christians stay away from public life in Jamaica, or refuse to see the relevance of their faith to their practice as politicians their political involvement becomes more corrupt. An interesting spiral circular logic results; the absence of their spirituality from their politics adds to its corruption, a corruption which they then use to justify the absence of their spirituality from their politics.

When we read the Bible as literature, and not as a doctrinal manual, it forces us to see concerns of the writers and their emphases. Such a reading paints a picture of the people of faith, with warts and foibles, trying to make sense of their godliness in a real world of tremendous difficulties. The Israelite midwives are forced to lie to Pharaoh to save the lives of new-born baby boys. Abraham lies to save his skin from the husband-killing culture of Egypt. Tamar tricks her father-in-law and has him impregnate her to "take the shame out of her eye." Rebecca is concerned for her son Jacob, who is largely ignored by his father, and so she concocts an elaborate plan to have the birth-right transferred to him. Rahab lies to her people, becoming a traitor, to save her life and that of her family. God instructs Samuel to lie to Saul when instructed to anoint David as king. The stories of the Bible paint a picture of people negotiating the difficult realities of every day, and in each case mentioned above, no one is judged. Why? Because they are forced to live in an unjust world, where the powerful tramples on the weak; the greater onus is on the powerful to change. It is understandable that the weak do less than what is expected since they are bartering for their lives. Yet, "the faith" which has been passed down to us chides the weak for their sinfulness while ignoring the powerful who create conditions for persons to lie and do less than the best to save their skins.

Perhaps then, this is the greatest difficulty I have with "the faith" that has been passed on: the biblical message that speaks to the establishment of a godly rule on earth, first given in Genesis and repeated throughout the scriptures, Old and New Testament, is ignored or treated as optional at best. We embrace elaborate times of prayer, worship and religious activity that are more akin to "the faith" condemned by every prophet of the Bible, including Jesus, and we ostracize those who see things differently. Yet our faith communities remain places of social exclusion, where the underclass and outcast find neither acceptance nor care.

Like Deitrich Bonhoeffer, I assert that "the faith" needs to be "de-religionized" that it can become useful for Christ in this world. After all "the faith" ought to be presenting us as "the visible presence of God on earth" through its incarnational contact with the world. Instead "the faith" has done nothing more than to attempt to "place new wine in old wineskins." "The faith" must die that people of faith can live as authentic witnesses in the world. But it dies hard, and so I choose to walk away from it. And so I declare that I am neither Brethren, Evangelical, Christian, Protestant nor Religious. I am David, trying to make sense of what it means to live as an authentic man in a crumbling world, touching the lives of people in authentic ways, helping them to live as authentic residents and neighbours, showing authentic love and concern for all. This is the faith that the Word encourages and which I seek to authentically embrace.

DISCUSSION QUESTIONS

1. Do you agree with the author's perspective that more often than not we do not "walk delicately on rice paper" but instead "drive bulldozers through a bed of roses" when dealing with those who find continuing in "the faith" difficult? To the extent that he is correct, why do we behave like that?

2. The author continually refers to "the faith" instead of "faith." What implication do you see in this? Do you then agree with him that one can walk away from "the faith" while still maintaining that faith is essential for making sense of reality?

3. What do you make of the idea that Christians are more often interested in their alignment to power instead of being servants? Is this a fair assessment of the state of the church? Explain.

4. Discuss the author's idea that "…'the faith' which has been passed down to us chides the weak for their sinfulness while ignoring the powerful who create conditions

for persons to live and do less than the best to save their skins?"

5. What does he mean when he says, "'The faith' must die that people of faith can live as authentic witnesses in the world?"

2.

CONTEXTUAL RELEVANCE

I have become a slave to all people to bring many to Christ. [1 Corinthians 9:19]

Once in recent times, I visited the Seventh Day Adventist Church nearest to my home. It was the first time in over forty years that I was attending a service in an Adventist Church. As a wee lad, I had attended while visiting with relatives in the country one summer. Since they were raised by a strict Adventist mother, my grand aunt, they all were required to attend church each Sabbath, though for most of my cousins that's where their commitment ended. Yet, as good family life dictated, each Sabbath morning we would walk the half mile to church, and as a boy not yet eight, I had to subject myself to the most boring two hours of my life. I conservatively estimate that it was two hours, but truth be told, it felt like about two weeks lost each time we went to the service. There was no joy whatsoever to be experienced, definitely not so for a boy of my age. On my more recent visit, the circumstances were different. My wife's nephew (12 years old) was visiting from Amsterdam, and his parents have brought up their family to be Seventh Day Adventists. I thought it hospitable to offer to take him to an Adventist Church since that is what he is most comfortable with. He was delighted at the offer, and so early one Sabbath morning we readied ourselves to attend service, beginning at 7:45 am. We walked the half mile down the road and got to the service on time, to be warmly greeted by persons awaiting the arrival of all, especially of visiting guests. I was in for a very interesting two and a half hours.

Andrews Memorial Seventh Day Adventist Church is a relatively popular church among Adventists in Kingston. It has a reputation for being a "society church" because of the perceived upper-crust of society that goes there. It is the home church of the wife of former Prime Minister, Bruce Golding, and a host of other famous Jamaicans. The Seventh Day Adventists make up the largest single church group in Jamaica, and so it might not be surprising to see various well-known persons in Jamaican society attending church there. The building itself is rather unremarkable in terms of modern church structures—it is very traditional in its appearance, with pews and pulpit just like any other traditional church. The worshipers themselves are traditionally dressed, with the average woman garbed in what we Sunday worshipers term their "Sunday best"—long ornate dresses and skirts, full sleeved blouses, and large Church hats. The average man is decked in a dark suit, a matching necktie, and nicely shined patented leather shoes. The King James Bible seems to be the preferred version here, and the songs.... (more on this later).

However, there are vestiges of modernity that are evident. The pews are softly cushioned, the sanctuary wonderfully air-conditioned (a fact that I took particular delight in since even at this time of the morning the day was already shaping up to be a scorcher), and various multi-media TV screens make following the words of hymns and sermon points rather easily. Thankfully, though I know many members of this church, no one recognized me at this service. I could sit in relative anonymity and do what I often do—observe, try to understand the culture, pay special attention to how the Bible was used, and of course make notes. I share with you some of my "findings."

Noah, my nephew, fell asleep at various times in the divine worship service, though compared to my experience back when I was a boy the service was not really long. I count this not as an indication of a deficiency in the church, since young boys when they are not up to trouble, do what they do best in church—sleep. It, however, did bring a question to my mind about church in general and how we make "divine worship" meaningful to the youngest among us. Surely there is value in having the family together, but what is it that we can do to make the time meaningful for our children? Of course, there was the "Children's Story Time" that was rather useful for those six years of age and under (perhaps in the way it was delivered). But I noticed that it did not connect to the theme of the morning, which had to do with Harvest. In any case, even during this story Noah found staying alert difficult. It was a good thing that I was taking notes since I myself am known to do some of my best sleeping in church.

My jotting and noting kept me awake, but I must confess that this was extremely difficult during the initial time of the singing of songs in preparation for worship. The songs were both old and culturally irrelevant to our Jamaican context. Again, this is nothing new to the church experience in Jamaica, but what I found particularly interesting was that the songs sung at Andrews sounded like they were largely from the White South of the USA. They reminded me more of a Blue Grass setting, and almost all were unfamiliar to me. And the choir was not good, much to my surprise. Yet the manner in which the faithful sang, and how they demonstrated their affection and appreciation for the music all around, was noteworthy. It's no different in most other churches, where we merely swap the music genre for some other, yet the songs, largely foreign to our context, get a resounding response from the faithful. But I need to ask: when will we begin to write our own songs from our own experiences with the Lord? I have been asking this question for many years now, but in this situation, I am not certain that the church adage that he who voices the concern must develop the answer would be a wise thing... unless the congregation does not mind singing strangely composed lyrics in the key of H flat or something else like that.

Perhaps the most significant thing of note to me was the use of the Bible in the two services that I stayed for (the Divine Worship and Sabbath School). There has been so much discussion over the years about Adventists' emphasis on their distinctive doctrines that I expected to hear about the importance of the Sabbath, the essential nature of food laws, or even the mysterious doctrine of Investigative Judgment. Not one mention was made of any such teaching while I was in church, and in fact what was conveyed from the pulpit and from Sabbath School

Cluster Leaders (I think that's what they were called) was in no way different from what you would hear in the typical, conservative Evangelical church.

The Preacher was very dynamic in his presentation, using various illustrations from the farm and the growing of various crops to make the point that before we reap we must put in a lot of effort in cultivating the field. After diligent work is done we can look forward to a bounteous harvest, if all the conditions are right. This, of course, was used to illustrate the passage from Luke 10 that the harvest is plenty but the labourers are few.

His point was crystal clear, but I could not help but wonder if his focus on tilling and planting the ground were a bit off kilter in speaking from this passage, which focuses on reaping. But who is going to quibble about such a minor point? Or is it really minor? Should not the real focus of Luke's gospel and its emphasis on the care for the outcast colour the preacher's understanding of sowing and reaping? I cannot remember any mention of this point, and I am left to wonder if indeed such preaching does not end up distorting the message of the Evangelist, and worse, the message of the Gospel itself? The preacher did not pay sufficient attention to the context in his preparation.

The very same pattern followed in Sabbath school, as groups reviewed their daily devotional lessons for the past week. The logistics of hosting these groups at Andrews are obviously very difficult, with all the groups remaining in the sanctuary, creating a constant buzz for the 45 minutes each leader is given to carry his group through the review. Only those closest to the leaders can sufficiently hear what he is saying, and so the only vocal participation comes from a few persons at the very front. I sat five rows from the leader and heard very few things that he said. But I noted that in what I heard there was little concern for the context of Acts 1:8, the focal point of the discussion at one point, and to tie in the church's harvest emphasis the point was made that God has empowered us to reap many souls for the kingdom.

Within the context of Luke's concern that spills over into his writing of Acts, this is not the major part of the teaching of the passage. But it is popular and well accepted, but how we read the Bible and how we conduct our discussions will give us little exposure to other, perhaps even more accurate readings. Neither Noah nor myself had an opportunity for significant participation apart from our attendance and attention—we both easily succeeded in the former but I think we struggled significantly with the latter.

I thank God for places like Andrews, because, in spite of the challenges I have mentioned, they have succeeded in cultivating a lifestyle among many of their people that redound to their personal benefit and the benefit of our nation. Some of the kindest and noblest people are to be found in institutions like this one, people who have made the life experiences of others more bearable, and even pleasant. Without their assistance, many of the people of our land would feed on a diet of hopelessness and despair.

My challenge, however, is two-fold: how might we make the worship experience more relevant to the context and circumstances of our people, and how might we read the Bible in its own context in a manner that will challenge our people to face the difficult realities of life in a manner that will truly promote the kingdom of God and themselves as subjects who bring hope and joy? This has got to be a concern of all our churches, be they SDA, Evangelicals, Pentecostals, Catholics, etc. Well, that's what I think.

DISCUSSION QUESTIONS

1. Should churches be really concerned about issues or "contextual relevance," or should they just be faithful in proclaiming the Gospel?

2. In the chapter the author speaks to a number of issues that he believes the Seventh Day Adventist Church needs. Identify and discuss any three? Should these be seen as concerns for only the SDAs? Explain.

3. He makes a big issue about the context of scripture being important if we are going to be really faithful to Biblical stories when preaching or teaching. Do you agree with him? Explain.

4. The author maintains that, in spite of his concern about the lack of relevance in how the churches present themselves, "they have succeeded in cultivating a lifestyle among many of their people that redound to their personal benefit and the benefit of our nation." Do you agree? How might this be possible, if indeed you agree?

5. The author mentions that his concern is twofold, "...how might we make the worship experience more relevant to the context and circumstances of our people, and how might we read the Bible in its own context in a manner that will challenge our people to face the difficult realities of life in a manner that will truly promote the kingdom of God and themselves as subjects who bring hope and joy?" How would you respond to those questions?

3.

Religion and Jamaican Elections

Let the words of my mouth, and the meditation of my heart, be acceptable in thy sight, O LORD, my strength, and my redeemer. [Psalm 19:14]

Portia Simpson-Miller quoted the words of Psalm 19 as she began her acceptance speech upon being elected Jamaica's 10th Prime minister, on the night of December 29, 2011. Her party, the People's National Party (PNP) had just been handed a resounding mandate over the Jamaica Labour Party (JLP) in national elections, by a margin of 41–22 seats in the House of Representatives.

For many, the victory was a surprise: for some because of the margin and for others because of the mere fact that the PNP won. That Mrs. Simpson-Miller would have begun with some reference to "the Lord" was expected, however, given the position that religion plays in the thinking of the average Jamaican as well as the fact that it is an entrenched part of our political culture. Very few people have commented on the use of religion in our elections, and I have been itching to do so, awaiting the appropriate time. But before I do so, let us remember the past.

Jamaican political parties have had a history of painting their fortunes as being in line with the Biblical ideal. Political mass meetings often have the feel of a "Gospel Meeting," with religious songs being used to whip the faithful into frenzy, as the stage is set for the "messianic-leader" to address them. Perhaps the best example of such a leader was Michael Manley, who was swept to power in 1972 on the idea that he was Joshua, taking the people into the Promised Land. He even had his "rod of correction," likened to the rod that was passed from Moses to Joshua as the latter took over the leadership of God's people as they went into the land of the Canaanites (I am almost sure there is no Biblical reference for such a transfer). At both victories of Michael Manley in the 1970's, and again in 1989 (as well as with the victories of the PNP in the 1990s—2002) a minister of religion would say a prayer of thanksgiving for the election victory.

Another significant election campaign, lavished with the imagery of the Bible, was that of the JLP of 1980, with its promise of "Deliverance is Near!" This time the Exodus of Israel from Egypt was the backdrop, and Edward Seaga was the new Moses who was to lead the people to freedom. If Manley were Joshua, Seaga was his superior, Moses. It seems significant that of all Jamaica's PM's since 1972, Seaga, as a sociologist specializing in folk religion, was the one who personally drew least on references to Christianity. Thus, overtly, the biblically infused campaign was more for rallying electoral support than to be a statement of some personal belief of the leader. PJ Patterson in the 1990s often campaigned on the need for the country to return to the Biblical values of love, honesty, and peace that we learned from our grandparents. He himself maintained membership in the Baptist church.

It is clear then that Jamaican politicians have used religion to rally mass support, whether or not religion really means more than that to them. However, the use of religion in the 2011 election campaign seemed even more sinister than it has ever been. Bruce Golding, the former Prime Minister and leader of the JLP, who was forced to step down after many difficulties associated with his connections to convicted drug lord, Christopher Coke, had walked the traditional religious lines in his campaigning, as Mrs. Simpson-Miller did. But Andrew Holness brought the use of religion, in my estimation, to a new low. Let me explain.

Of all the Prime Ministers Jamaica has had, Andrew Holness has been the one most overtly affiliated with a major Christian denomination. He is said to be an active member of the Seventh Day Adventist Church, the largest single denomination in Jamaica. Unconfirmed reports suggest that he is more than a mere church-goer, as he is reputed to be a Sabbath School teacher. In other words, he is a committed Adventist.

Many have raised concerns about the issue of how an Adventist Prime Minister would do the work of government on the Sabbath, but those who know the church realize that such is only from those who misunderstand Adventist teaching. After all, Adventist doctors and nurses still work on the Sabbath, doing good for humanity. "The Sabbath was made for man, not man for the Sabbath," so good and essential deeds must continue even then. In fact, God himself continues to work in sustaining the universe every day. But it is Mr. Holness's speech at a mass rally in Mandeville that formed the main plank of my concern, in addition to subsequent statements made by members of his party.

On December 4, 2011, thousands of the JLP party faithful were bussed to the Central Manchester capital of Mandeville, mainly with the promise of hearing the election date announced. At the meeting that night, Mr. Holness used the opportunity to remind the gathering of the ills of the PNP that formed the previous administration, warning that a return of the PNP to the government would be a disaster. All politicians do this, so this was not a surprise.

However, Holness anchored his speech around a number of deliberately distorted facts to make his point. The numbers of distortions are debated by many (some have counted up to fifteen), but what is known is that he misrepresented the facts about job-losses (claiming that there were none under the JLP when there were approximately 90,000), and about growth under the PNP (claiming that there was negative growth, when in fact there was a 3% growth over their period of governance). He is also reputed to have misled the country about "the bitter medicine to come" in 2012, which many maintained would entail further job losses in the public sector. This was due to the nature of the country's agreement with the IMF. Holness maintained that the "eucalyptus oil" that we would have to take was specifically speaking to the broadening of the tax net and not to job losses.

Now, it is the two actions of Holness following these distortions that concern us here—at the end of the speech he called the masses to prayer, and right there led them in an impassioned prayer for God's sanction and guidance on the party's move ahead. The next morning, when journalists asked him about the distortions he dismissed the concerns saying that people understood the essence of his message and were not caring about minor details as was now being mentioned. In other words, though he had "lied" and prayed that God would sanction those lies, people should not have been concerned about such. If such an intimation had come from a non-religious or even a merely religious person, it would not have been so alarming, but coming from a "committed Christian" it was disappointing, to say the least. Holness' stance made his faith a servant of his political ideals and not the other way around. In so doing he made his Christian convictions no more than chips to cash in when expedience dictated.

I suspect though, that for many Adventists listening to the speech, other things that he said were excruciating to the ears of the committed. His talk that his grandmother, who had administered eucalyptus oil to cure his maladies when he was young, was looking down from heaven and protecting him, wantonly trampled upon fundamental Adventist teaching that Holness himself knows. For one, the Adventist doctrine of "soul-sleep" means that there are none of our loved ones in heaven looking down on us. Additionally, to suggest that such a person protects us on our daily walk is to ascribe to Christianity what is believed to be the dastardly teaching of ancestral worship and petitioning spirits for protection. These might not have been Holness' intentions, but they certainly called into question the teachings of his church, or better yet, his own commitment to the teachings of his church, and all in the name of political expediency.

Sadly, prominent members of Holness's party then took the stand on subsequent occasions to use the Bible and Christianity to distort Portia Simpson-Miller's statement about the need for a review of the anti-buggery law, and then to bash the gay population. In all of this Holness remained publicly silent. Their impassioned claims of holiness and their fervent Bible bashing were seen for what they really were—merely a charade using Christianity to galvanize votes. Religion, and in particular Christianity, was called into question by Holness and his team in this election. This is one of the reasons why I think many Christians, in particular Adventists, might not have been so concerned that Andrew Michael Holness was defeated at the polls on the night of December 29, 2011. In fact, I believe that many Christians, Adventists in particular, were breathing a sigh of relief at the announcement of the results.

Since the election of 2011, Andrew Holness was once again returned to the Office of the Prime Minister, this time through popular vote and not by his party hierarchy to fill an empty slot. I cannot say that on this occasion Mr. Holness has been very vocal about matters of faith in support of his politics. What has been surprising to me is the silence of the Church in Jamaica on his previous distortions. No church publicly chided Mr. Holness or other politicians for their misuse of the religion, perhaps because they do not want to be branded as politically partisan. But, does not that failure to speak out at such abuse do more to distort the real nature of the faith, especially for those who are seeking understanding of these matters? We cannot stop persons from using our faith to seek to convince others, but at least we should be vocal about when they distort the same, even if, and especially when, we choose to support them for political office. This I believe is essential if we are going to develop a more responsible mind-set of those who are coming behind us.

DISCUSSION QUESTIONS

1. How should the Church respond to the general use of Christian spirituality by politicians to influence votes? Explain.

2. Do you agree with the idea that Andrew Holness's use of Christianity in that now infamous Mandeville mass-rally was in some senses worse than what other politicians have done in the past? Explain.

3. Our Churches have generally remained outside of political discussions, especially during elections, as a way of remaining impartial in matters of party politics in the eyes of the public. What are some of the advantages and disadvantages of this stance?

4. The writer maintains that the Church's failure to speak out against the abuse of the Christian message by politicians to influence votes only helps to distort the message of Gospel. What are your thoughts on this?

5. We have for a long time lamented the dirty nature of party politics. How might conscientious Christians get involved in

the political process without getting sullied by it? Is that even desirable or recommended? Explain.

4.

CHRISTIANITY, HEAVEN, AND EARTH

May your Kingdom come soon. May your will be done on earth, as it is in heaven. [Matthew 6:10]

A friend of mine, in commenting on the reparations debate that our country is currently engulfed in, laments the ill-thinking of the British who continue to treat others as though they are less than human. She pointed out the fact that, having made so much money on the backs of the enforced enslavement of our people, the British also gave us a religion that promises us everything in the afterlife and nothing material now. It is that last sentiment that got me thinking, as much as I am interested in the question of reparations.

In a lecture at the college in which I teach, the Hon. Omar Davies, the then Minister of Transport and Works, commented on the "looking to the afterlife" as a part of Christianity that he has found inferior to other religious understandings of human hope, in particular, Rastafari. Davies opines that the theology of postponed justice, as seen in various Christian hymns, is the single greatest stumbling block for him personally, and for the black man generally, in accepting Christianity as being viable. I responded to him, showing that though the sentiment is evident in many Christian hymns, the Bible that Christians hold as their manifesto, does not countenance such an understanding, even if it supports the idea of ultimate justice in the afterlife. Biblical writers, one after the other, speak of the importance of justice now, especially for the most marginalized of our people. Davies's response was quite interesting —"Christianity is as Christianity does."

I say that Davies's response was interesting simply because I do not believe that he would add the same type of reasoning to any of his own professions. Let me explain: Davies himself has been associated with various churches who are not guilty of the accusation he levels at Christianity, though we may conclude that many are guilty as charged. If the behavior (or belief) of the many is indicative of the relative value of the whole, and if indeed the perceived prevalence of a devalued appreciation for justice in the here and now is a necessary disqualification of the value of Christianity, should the same level of reasoning not be brought to bear on the value of other professions, institutions or even individuals? Take, for instance, politicians; it is a common belief that politicians are more interested in "feathering their own cap" than really working for the wellbeing of the people whom they serve. Does that common notion, and indeed prevalent evidence, disqualify the value of politics and politicians? Or is it indicative of a greater need for re-education and redirection of the efforts of all involved? I think the answer to that is quite evident.

So, let me set the record straight, or as straight as I can do so in such a limited space. My desire is that we, especially those of us who call ourselves Christian, evaluate our beliefs and practices to see if the Christianity we speak of and do is one that squares with the Biblical teaching on the matter of creating a just society where the most vulnerable are protected. I will seek to outline my ideas in a few, clearly stated points.

First, the Bible is filled with teachings that point to a concern for social justice on this side of eternity. The books of Amos and Micah in the Old Testament are just two of the myriad offerings on the matter, which is first laid down in the Pentateuch. See Deuteronomy 15, for instance.

Second, the Bible does teach that because of human failing, in spite of our best efforts we will not achieve a perfect society on this side of eternity. As such, especially among the New Testament writers, there is a longing for the Second Coming of Christ, where all will be made perfect once again. However, in stating that, it does suggest that the greater we work at the practice of love and justice (the ethics of the kingdom of God) here and now is the more we will see such on the earth. The kingdom of God is like leaven. When a small amount is kneaded into the dough it will eventually impact the whole batch (Matthew 13:33). It, therefore, leaves Christians with the decided responsibility to do our best to be the spreaders of that kingdom of love and justice (Matthew 23:23). See also Mark and Luke for an abundance of teaching on this matter.

Third, where then did Christianity get this idea of looking to heaven and ignoring earth? This unbiblical teaching is largely the result of a "missionary Christianity" that was brought to the Caribbean between the fifteenth–eighteenth centuries, and which was more concerned with shoring up a class structure that would provide a steady stream of servants for white society. When the "natives" were finally "allowed" to have souls, it was important to teach a kind of divine order on this side of eternity, with the promise of great rewards on the other side depending on upholding the codes that governed this side.

Thus, the black man's lot as the "drawer of water" and "hewer or wood" was a divine test that he could pass if he readily accepted his lot here and now, and which he would be handsomely rewarded for if he did well on those duties.

Fourth, that teaching has so taken root in the church over the years, that though the missionaries and slavery have long gone, it remains in the church as sacrosanct teaching. Any attempt to get many Christians to even begin thinking of the error is greeted with accusations "worldliness" and "lack of faith." So, without even bothering to understand the history of how this teaching has developed in the church, many Evangelical and Pentecostal churches today continue to deny their responsibilities for the here and now as they seek to prepare for heaven. In the meantime, the most vulnerable in society continue to face the most difficult challenges for basic survival, challenges that might just be more easily overcome if the collective effort of the church was channeled towards solutions.

In light of the above, I think I can firmly assert in agreement with Bob Marley and the Wailers (in particular Peter Tosh) that I am *"sick and tired of your ism schism game / Die and go to heaven in Jesus' name."* I wish that many more of us would just begin to read the Bible and see that in it lies a revolutionary blueprint for living that if we were to begin to put it in practice, our world would be such a better place.

One of the things that disappointed me about Dr. Davies's statement was that an essential part of the success of the community in which he serves as a Member of Parliament is the concerted effort of two churches to deal with the issues of social injustice faced by the people. Inner Cities for Christ and Praise City International are congregations led by ministers that have used their every resource to help persons get an education, skills, and jobs, or establish businesses, which will lead them into lives of greater independence and responsibility.

Both the churches emphasize preparation for the afterlife, but neither ignores its responsibility for helping establish the kingdom of God in the here and now. Maybe Davies had other things in mind, but he really ought to have mentioned the work of these churches, and others like them, as a more responsible Christianity to be emulated than to dismiss the whole religion as lacking. He would never sanction our denial of the value of all politicians based on the common practice of politicians to care for themselves at the expense of their people.

Christianity might indeed teach a denial of justice in the here and now (if, like Omar Davies, we agree that Christianity is as Christianity does), as too many churches are disconnected from the realities in which our people live and suffer through. But most certainly, if we understand Christianity as the religion of the Bible, then what many of our churches practice is most definitely not Christianity. *I encourage us all to read the Bible, that when we critique the actions of Christians we will do so with a better understanding of what the Bible states that they ought to be doing.* That is an ongoing challenge that we face if we are to remain relevant as we offer hope to our people in the here and now, even as we prepare for the afterlife.

DISCUSSION QUESTIONS

1. In an earlier chapter the writer states, "Like Deitrich Bonhoeffer, I assert that 'the faith' needs to be *de-religionized* that it can become useful for Christ in this world." How do you think this statement compares with Dr. Davies's concern about the Church?

2. What are your thoughts on the author's response to Dr. Davies's assertion that the Church, as seen in its racist hymns, is irrelevant to the realities of the Jamaican (Caribbean) person? Explain. What steps might it take to become more relevant in your view?

3. Can the Church really prepare for the afterlife while focusing on the concerns for justice for the outcast in this life? Is it still the Church if it fails to do so?

4. The author asserts, *"I encourage us all to read the Bible, that when we critique the actions of Christians we will do so with a better understanding of what the Bible states that they ought to be doing."* Do you

agree with him here? Or do you see dangers in this suggestion? Explain.

5. Reflect on the poem, "Contextual Page Rage" that appears in the introduction to Section I. Do you think it accurately captures what needs to be a correction of a "cock-eyed" vision of the Gospel? Explain your response.

PART 2:
THE CHURCH IN COMMUNITY

COME...

Why should we listen to you,
When we despise your pomposity,
Which so easily dismisses us
With your easy pronouncements?
Why should we seek out your succour,
When you continue to ignore our reality,
Willfully styling us as evil all too easily,
Without ever considering our circumstance?
We hate you and your announcements!

Come unto me all ye who are burdened,
Come to me ye heavily laden... I will give rest.
Come take my yoke upon yourselves.
Come...my yoke is light, my burden is best.

Will you provide answers
When our only way is the sale of ourselves?
Women having to enter easy transactions
Without a thought for basic dignity;
Wicked men purchasing sensual rides
With the teenage daughters of their friends,
Wantonly robbing them of youth and
    innocence,
Wrecking any possibility of a decent future.
Why should we listen to you?

Come unto me all ye who are burdened,
Come to me ye heavily laden...I will give rest.
Come take my yoke upon yourselves.
Come...my yoke is light, my burden is best.

We the men of this wounded land,
Wearily hear your droning emptiness,
When will this evil cycle end?
What hope is there for us who desire better?
Why should we believe when your shepherds
    too are thieves?
Whittling away at our meagre meal time
    provisions,
Wrestling from us our wives, daughters, and if
    you could, sons
Without ever speaking to us as the lords of
    our homes?
We want to believe that you speak the truth,
    but do you?

Come unto me all ye who are burdened,
Come to me ye heavily laden...I will give rest.
Come take my yoke upon yourselves.
Come...my yoke is light, my burden is best.

In recent years the Church in the Caribbean has taken a bashing from thinkers who have come to champion a "post-Christian" world, free from religious intrusion. Christianity and its message is painted as irrelevant, and Christians are often described in derogatory terms for maintaining their faith. Though much of the criticism is warranted it is the substantive message of the transforming power of the Gospel that keeps many sticking with the faith and a constant flow of seekers coming week after week, desperately wanting meaning in their lives. The Church ought not to be shy about its message, even as it seeks to make itself a better witness. The gospel is still, "the power of God unto the salvation, of everyone who believes (Romans 1:16)." There is nothing irrational or irrelevant about the gospel, and we must eagerly share it in all its fullness with a dying and decaying world.

5.

CHURCH IN THE COMMUNITY

So God created human beings in his own image. In the image of God he created them; male and female he created them. [Genesis 1:27]

In so-called Christian countries, like Jamaica where I live, the Church is constantly under the microscope, especially as our society continues the downward spiral into lawlessness. Recent apparent increased abductions, rapes and murders of children and the elderly have caused a firestorm of debate nationwide. As I write the country's parliament is taking a conscience vote as to whether or not capital punishment is to be retained on our law books, with most parliamentarians seemingly ready to back the desires of their constituents—namely, not only to retain the death penalty, but to speedily resume the execution of murderers as a means of stemming the rot that has set into our society. In all of this many are pointing an accusing finger at the Church, as they believe that for too long there has been a greater concern with "self-preservation" on the part of Pastors and denominational captains, than on the social and moral upbringing of our people and communities.

What we cannot deny is that in spite of the rumblings in society, and the malaise that has set in in many churches, there are many others that are enjoying record attendances. And there are not only a few such churches in our land. Yet many of the communities in which these churches exist are themselves examples of the worse poverty imaginable, where people are asked each day to sacrifice families, friends, neighbours and themselves for less than a basic survival. How can these churches continue to exist in such circumstances, happily praising God without a thought for addressing the reality in which many of their own people live?

One of the first problems is that the churches seem to believe that their greater responsibility lies elsewhere. I have arrived at this conclusion from a mini-survey done by some of my students at the Jamaica Theological Seminary (JTS) where I lecture. Ten of my students, representing eight different denominations, each did a recorded report of sermons in their churches over a twelve week period, to evaluate the community conscience and care that came forth as a challenge to believers. In the approximately 100 surveys collected from the ten churches, only two had anything to do with the community, a mere 2%. Instead, the vast majority was concerned with issues such as "overcoming spiritual struggles", "standing on God's promises", "leading others to the Lord", "avoiding sexual immorality", and such the like.

Our people have adopted an all too personal and private understanding of a relationship with God and in so doing have neglected the community. When we do this we become guilty of the very thing Jesus chided the religious leaders of his day for: "...you tithe dill, mint, and cummin, but have neglected the weightier matters of the Law: love, justice and mercy" (Matt 23:23). The weightier matters do require a personal commitment on the part of all Christians, but they can only be enacted in community. When these become our focus then indeed we will see a more relevant Church, involved as a part of the solution to our society's disintegration, instead of our standing on the periphery shouting irrelevant platitudes.

But our churches might not be as involved in community because our leaders do not know how to be. Some may have accomplished much in years gone by, but most, right now, seem to be accomplishing very little in terms of community transformation. For a long time, they have been on the periphery, maybe enjoying a mere modicum of success, if any at all. Now, our community realities require a different approach and our churches do not know how to respond. It's like driving a standard shift car for years, where your left foot serves only for the clutch. If you were to change to a Go-cart where there is no clutch, your left foot is there to operate the brakes. Adjusting to this is such a difficult task, that some persons never bother with Go-carts after one try. Unfortunately, as difficult as effective community ministry might be, our churches cannot opt-out of it.

How do we become more relevant to our communities? The first thing to realize is that we are not speaking primarily about more relevant programmes as much as we speak about a more relevant mindset. Programmes are known to be notoriously contextually sensitive, that is they work in some contexts and not in others. But a more relevant mindset (a contextual one) will keep various principles in mind and will continue to devise programmes that will then seek to minister effectively according to these principles. What are some of these? Do not be surprised that their foundation is Biblical. This is what sets the Church apart from other social agencies, and is her very raison-d'etre.

1. All men (not just Christians) are created in the image and likeness of God. The worst offenders in our communities are themselves God's image bearers.

2. Sin has tarnished that image in man, and in every case is seeking some opportunity to further denigrate man. Thus, sin is dastardly, not merely because it offends God's sensibilities, but because it destroys God's creation, hence offending his sensibilities.

3. One of the main ways in which sin manifests itself is through our need to show ourselves better than others. Mankind uses every means possible to put down others and elevate self: sex, gender, race, class, politics, religion, profession, wealth, education, employment, etc. Our communities are rife with these sins, even when sexual sins are non-existent, a fact overlooked by many of our churches.

4. Jesus Christ died to restore God's image in man, and the relationship between God and man. Those who have experienced a restored relationship with God are now responsible for addressing issues in the social order that continue to denigrate

God's creation. This responsibility is not popular among many but is essential to our lives of renewed minds encouraged in Romans 12:2. The previous verse indicates that anything else is worldliness.

If our churches keep the above in mind, what issues will they see in their communities that need addressing? I suggest that leaders and followers alike discuss these things and identify situations that need attention and then work at them. Some may require long-term effort, like the re-socializing of our youth. Quick fixes might do for others, like helping to repair someone's roof. In all cases what will be required is a new way of seeing each individual, as a special child of God requiring all the love of God that believers can show.

When we think like this relevant programmes become easier to identify, as well as the expertise required for effectively implementing them. This opens up possibilities for us to involve more believers in ministry, according to their abilities, and to train them for the most effective use of those abilities. Surely, as they get more involved a more meaningful bond between them and the people of our communities will be created. But everything begins with a change of mindset. In a nutshell, the people of our communities are

bearers of the image of God, battered by the rav-
ages of sin. The church must be involved in an
attempt to restore the luster to that image, by
tackling sin and its effects, wherever such becomes manifest.

But, is it the Church's responsibility to seek for
social change and/or reform? This is perhaps the
single most asked question by conservative
Christians when the issue of Church and community involvement comes up. As far as these
well-thinking believers see it, the Church has a
spiritual responsibility and ought not to be side-
tracked by social concerns, as urgent as those
might be. We elect governments to see to the
physical and social well-being of the community;
the Church ought to care for the spiritual.

Undoubtedly, the Church does have a spiritual
concern, and merely thinking socially does not
address that concern. However, if we divorce the
physical and social from the spiritual, we have
missed the full essence of the Biblical message,
as I have argued above. Of significant concern
now is from where this dichotomy has come, to
the extent that it is the dominant way of thinking
for so many Christians today. It seems to me that
this dichotomized spirituality is as a result of the
fact that our former colonial masters were the
ones who brought us the Christian message. In
England, even in the heyday of slavery, this strict

separation between the social and spiritual was not a reality in the Anglican Church. In fact, the Church of England was, in the minds of many thinkers, a mere change in name and titular head, when compared to the Roman Catholic Church that it replaced. As the Roman Catholic Church was the final authority on all matters spiritual and social, so was the Anglican Church in England. How then did this change in the Caribbean?

Historical evidence suggests that when the Anglican Church established itself in the West Indies in the mid 1600's (see Arthur Dayfoot— *The Shaping of the West Indian Church*) as a means to minister to the British Plantation owners and operators, they soon found it pragmatic to separate their spiritual message from that of the social responsibilities of their followers, as a means of keeping the financial support of these said followers.

The government in England had told the Church in the West Indies that they would not be supporting her financially, and so created the Parish system where taxes levied on the planters looked after the social and spiritual welfare of the colonies. Apparently, the church leaders believed it expedient not to overly trouble the planters about the social misbehaviours, fearing their withholding of taxes, which would lead to the church's demise. As such, in a fairly short time, the church's message was limited to the spiritual, to the extent that there was not even a community centre present on any church property. The buildings were only seen as places of worship.

What began as expediency for the survival of the Church soon became binding law, and later non-conformist churches that came (Methodists, Moravians, Presbyterians, etc.) found themselves operating in these strictures in order to be allowed to maintain a presence here. Apparently, this was the pattern of the establishment of Christianity wherever the colonial masters went, to the extent that we have had a large number of Christians growing up in such contexts where today they themselves defend the idea that as long as the soul is alright for the afterlife, we need not be overly bothered by the social realities in which we live. They know no other theology.

Unfortunately, these same Christians scoff at theology and theological education, saying that such amounts to nothing more than man's perverse ideas of the Bible. They strongly believe that their ideas are taken only from the Bible. But if they were to take off the denominational lenses they have inherited, and read the Bible cover to cover, they would see that though the spiritual is not the same as the social, it is almost impossible to maintain the spiritual without a serious concern for the social. The challenge is for them to take up any book of the Bible, and attempt to read it without bias. I guarantee that they will see that a dichotomy does exist between the spiritual and the social, but not in the Bible. Such exists only in the minds of people who have been conditioned to see it just that way, simply because it was sinfully beneficial to others. And that dichotomy continues today, simply because it remains sinfully beneficial to some.

Our churches today constantly need to revisit their Biblical mandates and attitudes as a means of making themselves more relevant to the lives of the people of their communities. Anything else threatens to freeze them in time and space and leaves them on the outside of the evolving lives of their people. This is one sure way of keeping our churches locked in irrelevancy and deny our people the opportunity to experience the full transforming impact of the Gospel of Jesus Christ in their lives.

DISCUSSION QUESTIONS

1. The Church operates with the mind-set that its greater responsibility lies with a concern for issues of personal and private salvation than with issues of community transformation—do you agree with this assessment? Is that bad or good?

2. How does any Church continue with an emphasis on the spiritual, with little notice of issues of social justice in light of passages like Micah 4:8 and Matthew 23:23? Do you think these verses lay down a clear responsibility for the Church to be involved in justice issues? Explain.

3. The writer asserts that one of the reasons why Churches are not as involved in their communities as they ought to be is simply because their leaders do not know how to be involved. Do you agree? What do you make of his idea that what is required is not a new programme but a new mind-set? Explain.

4. In the chapter the writer speaks about the "dichotomized message of Christianity," which had its origin in ideas of self-

preservation by the colonial masters and not the teachings of scripture. How did this idea first strike you when you read it?

5. "It is almost impossible to maintain a spiritual concern without a serious concern for the social." Is this idea even Biblical? If it is, on what basis can the Church continue without focussing on such issues?

6.

CARMEL AND THE GOSPEL

For this is how God loved the world: He gave his one and only Son, so that everyone who believes in him will not perish but have eternal life. [John 3:16]

I once had the privilege of speaking at a youth camp, over the long Easter Weekend, put on by Carmel Gospel Hall from Eastern Kingston. The camp brought together over 80 young people, aged 14–30 (there was 2 closer to 50), most from the volatile Rockfort community. For over fifty years Carmel has faithfully declared the message of the saving grace of Jesus Christ and continues to do so among a people racked by violence, destitution, and division, as well as the deep cynicism of some who view the church as opportunistic, uncaring and weak. Despite the difficulties, the leadership remains faithfully committed to its task, which viewed up-close translates into a deep commitment to the people of Rockfort. My time at Carmel camp profoundly cemented my thoughts that the Gospel is essential for our people and that the Gospel is indeed profoundly more than has been most often presented to us.

Christians speak of the Gospel being "the good news that Jesus Christ has died for our sins." This has put us in a right relationship with God, which means that we can look forward to an eternity with God in His perfect heaven. Sadly, I have struggled with why this is "good news," since it requires me to die (physically) first to benefit from it. Of course, the vast majority of Christians will immediately see that the Gospel is much more than this, but most cannot explain it in better terms, or at least they have not bothered to try. The brief, popular definition is at best incomplete, but unfortunately, it is the incompleteness of the definition that has limited the ministry of the Church and stymied Christian responsibility as it is worked out in the real world of living before we face physical death. The Carmel experience over that long weekend helped me clarify my thoughts. I desire to share them by looking at the experiences of two of the characters at camp.

Breads was a happy go lucky young man; a self-proclaimed football star and "girls' man", moved by a sense of fashion and style; he idled through school as many young men do today. But unlike many other young men from average

everyday homes, Breads had another character-
istic that many people feared. He was related to
known "Shottas" (gun-men) in the community.
After school, he got a job with a large manufac-
turing company supplying goods to a wide variety of supermarkets. Breads found that he could
easily "top-up" his salary by an ingenious
scheme of stealing the very goods he delivered
to the supermarkets, without them knowing (details withheld). This he did as a way of life,
though in hindsight he had no need to, since
even his salary he was not spending to meet his
needs. Other activities cared for these. Then a
series of events caused him to consider the Gospel and to seek a change in his life.

Like many other young men in the community,
Breads had spent many years in Carmel's Boys'
Club, where he was engaged by members of the
church through sports, as they shared the message of Jesus and sought to help the youngsters
in many other ways. He played the sports, went
to Sunday school, and at the right time (as most
people did) left to pursue life (early teens). His
waywardness increased as described earlier,
with no thought to follow through on the messages the church had presented to him. But one
day all that changed. On that day a relative called
him and gave him a gun to keep. He promptly
pushed it in his waist and went on the street,

feeling larger than life. As fate would have it, at that precise moment a police patrol was driving through the community, and spotting them Breads leaned against a wall and pretended that he was just standing innocently. Miraculously, the police patrol drove on without stopping. He rushed home and put down the gun.

Later that evening, at a near-by dance, a friend of his was sitting on a wall, when a "gun salute" for an artist went horribly wrong, killing him right where he was. A little later news broke that Steve "Shorty" Malcolm and Theodore Whitmore, two famous Reggae Boyz, were returning to Montego Bay after a match at the National Stadium when their car crashed killing Shorty.

Breads wondered about these three events and for the first in a long time, he took a closer look at his life. He was not yet ready to die as he had not yet found purpose, nor was he living in any way beneficial to anyone. So he sought out Cleston "Uncle Clarry" Green (from the Boys' Club) the first chance he got, and after hounding him to show that he was really serious about his desire, he became a Christian.

Today, a number of years later, Breads is the youth leader at Carmel, married with a child, and having a profound impact on many of the hope-less youth who live in the community. Through the encouragement of the leadership, he has returned to school and is living a model life, though still residing in the Rockfort community.

Uncle Clarry himself also has a tremendous testimony. He also grew up in the Rockfort community and was living a dangerously aimless life, much too close to guns, wanted men and divisive politics. One of his mentors repeatedly and earnestly warned him against associating with the church, since the church was filled with thieves. In 1980, Clarry, still a youth, accepted an invitation to attend Easter Camp with Carmel, though he was never involved with the church. He hid the fact from his mentor and proceeded to camp, where on the first night he and two friends broke out and went to a "Go-Go" club since they were in no way interested in the spiritual direction of the camp. But on Resurrection Sunday night Clarry was gripped by the message in the Chapel session and could not move. That night he chose the Gospel and was reborn, much to the anger of his mentor who refused to speak with him after hearing of his conversion.

One day, Clarry's former mentor stormed into the churchyard where Clarry was engaging in a Bible study, placed a gun in his lap in full view of everyone, and commanded him to take back the gun and leave Church. Clarry resolutely refused, and as we say, the rest is history. His life was turned around to the point where he began to make it a success, eventually got a job in sales, got married, bought a home, and is today one of the pastors at Carmel. He has carried on the ministry of the Boys' Club, which has broadened its reach in the community to the extent where almost every boy in the community at one time or another has been touched by its efforts. Clarry today enjoys "protected person status" and like the other leaders at Carmel has free passage any-where in this volatile community. He continues to make a difference in the lives of many.

What is it that I am saying about the Gospel from these two stories? The message that our sins are forgiven through Jesus, when understood in context, also says to us that the disqualifications that come with modern community living are never considered in God's mind. Despite the "badness" of men, or whatever other maladies they show, God's love reaches out to them be-cause to God they are worth much. No life is bey-ond redemption, even when we have lost hope and pray that some die. In Christ Jesus, there is neither Jew nor Greek, bond or free, male or fe-male—or in our parlance no righteous or sinner, no rich or poor, no man or woman. The good news is that disqualifiers do not count against us with God, even if they do in our communities.

I suspect that most Christians reading this will agree with the above, even if they do not fully understand the ramification of their agreement. There is more to the Gospel than this, more that is blatantly clear but often overlooked in today's church. God empowers those He saves to make a profound impact on their world in the here and now, not just through their spiritual message, but through their practical involvement in the community.

Churches that preach while remaining on the outside of the lives of the people who hear their message, are not only limiting the impact of that message but are actually distorting it. Often, what is communicated is that people remain in the mire in which they find themselves, simply because they are disobedient, wanting their own way. If they would only just show faith, their lives would become better, but they refuse to do so because of some fault with them. With that comes the subtle truth that the church refuses to be involved in people's everyday struggles because it has rejected them in some way or another. The church then is seen as standing in stark contrast to the message it proclaims from the platform. We preach that God loves everyone, but we fail to show a concerned love to many.

When we get involved in the lives of our people we will see that the hopelessness that often keeps them prisoners is more than spiritual in nature. Poverty, lack of education, political victimization and a host of other debilitating factors are a band of robbers keeping our communities in bondage. Christians, even when they live in these communities, seem to more easily overcome these challenges than others, when they receive wide-ranging support from fellow believers. Presenting the Gospel to non-Christians should be no different, as full, godly involvement in people's lives is not optional. The Gospel demands such because it is the good news of salvation to everyone who believes—the good news of shalom: peace, wholeness, well-being. The church needs to rediscover the fullness of its message, and develop many more Carmels that hopelessness will one day become alien to our communities.

How do you understand the Gospel?

DISCUSSION QUESTIONS

1. Two Churches minister in the same community of tremendous social neglect; one is deeply involved in the total lives of members of the community, while the other maintains a distinctly "spiritual" emphasis. Is one more faithful to the message of the Gospel than the other? Explain.

2. "The traditional definition of the Gospel as "the good news that Jesus Christ has died for our sins" ...is at best incomplete, but unfortunately, it is the incompleteness of the definition that has limited the ministry of the Church and stymied Christian responsibility as it is worked out in the real world..." Do you agree? Explain.

3. "God empowers those He saves to make a profound impact on their world in the here and now, not just through their spiritual message, but through their practical involvement in the community." If this is so would an authentic Christian make a better witness in the community from which he or she is from? Explain.

4. We may assume that the writer is correct when he says, "Despite the 'badness' of men, or whatever other maladies they show, God's love reaches out to them because to God they are worth much. No life is beyond redemption, even when we have lost hope and pray that some die." If so, how might the Church target those in the community who are thought of as being downright "bad?" Ought it to do so?

5. How might the Church "rediscover the fullness of its message, and develop many more Carmels that hopelessness will one day become alien to our communities?" Is that even possible, though?

7.

LOVING GOD WITH MY WHOLE BEING

You must love the Lord your God with all your heart, all your soul, and all your mind.
[Matthew 22:37]

My wife and I were in a bookstore in Kingston on New Year's Eve attempting to purchase ear-phones. The store had on display some small, new-fangled musical gizmo that belted out a YouTube video in a manner that belied its size. The whole store was filled with the powerful voice of Tasha Cobbs declaring the power in the name of Jesus to break every chain. I was struck by the intensity with which Cobbs blasted her lyrics in the never-ending version (38 minutes) being played. One of the store clerks commented her disapproval of Cobbs's grating scream in her oft-repeated declaration, "I hear the chains falling!" She was not sure why Christians had to scream out their throats to show their commitment to the Lord. But Cobbs's song does move people. The video was one of her live performances in church, which has fetched close to twenty million views, and it ends with an altar call to which hundreds stream forward to have their "chains broken."

There is no doubt that we Caribbean folk are largely an emotional people. There are many things we do with gusto or we do not do them at all. We play hard and we work hard as long as we want to play or work; we celebrate intensely when our team wins (just check Half-Way-Tree Square when Usain wins at a major championship) and show sheer disgust when they lose; and we pursue our relationships with passion, and many of us end them with passion—especially men who hate being dumped by their women.

The rising incidents of intense domestic violence ending with the deaths of our sisters are evidence that our emotional nature is often not tempered by reason, leading to our lack of will to passionately do that which is right when things are going against us. In that bookstore, it suddenly hit me that this was a picture of the way many of us display our faith in church. We passionately belt out our commitment to God in the loudest and most sustained praise; at the same time for too many, there is not a similar fervency in logically considering and doing what the Gospel requires.

Now, I must be truthful—the above descriptions do not speak of me, or the few like me. Of course, we are passionate about various things in our lives, however, when it comes on to the things of God our passions are driven intellectually rather than by the emotions. We want to know the reason behind everything and are put off when preachers twist the scriptures to make grand statements from the Bible. It's troubling that as long as these preachers make their statements with gusto they can be assured of the loudest "Amen," the most tears of commitment, and fervent commendation.

An unthinking approach to the scriptures has become standard in many of our congregations, and the preacher that brings more than a modicum of intellect to his messages demonstrates that the Spirit of God does not reside with him. I have subjected many to such spiritless deliveries, and I have become aware that persons often politely greet me after a sermon, apparently wishing that they will not need to sit through more than five minutes of another one of my intellectual drivels. Not all persons are as diplomatic, however, especially the seven-year-old boy who spoke with me after I delivered a message at a New Testament Church of God. Let me tell you about it.

The Pastor of that church just happened to be one of my students. We had great times in class discussions, and he probably mistakenly believed that I would have something to say to challenge his congregation. He wanted me to speak from Joel 2 (I remember the passage but not the theme), and I diligently prepared myself for the assignment. I started off well, greeting the people in the style to which they are accustomed, and then launching off with a good ice-breaker and joke that had them laughing. All was going well (for a full three minutes) until I began to explain the nuance of a word from the passage to draw an implication for us.

For the next twenty-five minutes, I was speaking to myself, as the church was deathly silent. People passing on the outside might have been wondering what was happening on the inside since there was hardly a sound coming from the usually rocking church whose loud-speakers blared out the music and message. At the end, my student took the mike and suddenly turned my sermon into an emotional delight for the people, just by taking one point and preaching it over for five minutes.

Suddenly, the altar was packed with supplicants. As I stood alone outside after the service a little boy, no more than seven years of age, came over to me with a big smile and a word of admonition; "Bwoy, you need some spirit man!" With that, he laughed and walked away.

I have long ago resolved in my mind that I will not be who I am not, especially when delivering God's word. Like Paul (1 Corinthians 2:1-5), I have sought to make the Word of God the centre-stage of my deliveries:

1 And so it was with me, brothers and sisters. When I came to you, I did not come with eloquence or human wisdom as I proclaimed to you the testimony about God. 2 For I resolved to know nothing while I was with you except Jesus Christ and him crucified. 3 I came to you in weakness with great fear and trembling. 4 My message and my preaching were not with wise and persuasive words, but with a demonstration of the Spirit's power, 5 so that your faith might not rest on human wisdom, but on God's power.

Paul's style was not to everyone's liking. Some at Corinth were not swayed by his preaching, as Paul himself declared in 2 Corinthians 10:10 —"For some say, 'His letters are weighty and forceful, but in person he is unimpressive and his speaking amounts to nothing.'" If the great Apostle Paul, the greatest theologian in the history of the Christian church, was subject to such criticism, why should I think that it should be any different for me? I have resolved to continue in my delivery of the word in the best way I know, and I will not be moved by people's response as long as I am faithful to the text. The use of the intellect has got to be seen as more important than being swayed by the emotions when we claim that we love God—or is it?

Systematic Theologians of yesteryear, in their discussion of the person of the Holy Spirit, often declared that the Holy Spirit is a "he" (a person) and not an "it" (a thing or a force). They sought to demonstrate this by showing that the Holy Spirit has all the characteristics of a person, just like the Father and the Son: He has intellect (He knows, as in Romans 8:26), emotions (He can be grieved, as in Ephesians 4:30), and will (He carries out the purposes of God, as in 2 Peter 1:21). As I thought about that it occurred to me that in us all three components of person-hood are expected to serve God since everything we are ought to be used for Him.

I have pitted the intellect against the emotion, but how does the will figure in all of this? The answer came to me easily: *I must use my will to understand God and subject my emotions to honour him that in everything I obey him.* It was shortly after coming to this realization that I heard about William Temple's famous quote on worship:

To worship is to quicken the conscience by the holiness of God, to feed the mind with the truth of God, to purge the imagination by the beauty of God, to open the heart to the love of God, to devote the will to the purpose of God.

Surely, God wants us to understand His Word, and so we need more persons who are diligent in the disciplines of exegesis and hermeneutics to ensure that they have "rightly divided" it. The stakes are too high when we have the Word distorted from the platform, leading many astray. But God also wants us to serve Him with passion and enthusiasm, since that is how we pursue almost everything else meaningful to us. Without fervor in our service we are communicating that it is not very important to us. In the end both those poles (the pursuit of the intellect and the emotions) are not opponents but teammates making the third pole possible, that of doing the will of God. If others ought to develop their intellectual bent to honour God then those like me must develop our emotions for the same goal. It is the only way we are going to see God's will transforming our nature, as we bring His truth to passionately address the things in our land that do not honour His will.

DISCUSSION QUESTIONS

1. The writer intimates that the Caribbean Christian is generally more swayed by the emotional appeal of Church than the intellectual engagement. Do you agree with this statement? If so, what are the advantages and disadvantages of such a reality?

2. What explains this general lack of intellectual rigour in addressing the issues of God in the Church? How might we address it?

3. Ought we to be really concerned about those in our Churches who find an emotional display of their spirituality difficult? How might we constructively help them?

4. Could you identify the ministries in your Church that consciously and specifically develop the intellectual, emotional, and volitional responsibilities of Christians? How do these ministries do it? Are they actually effective in the methodologies they use? How might they improve?

5. "I must use all my will to understand God and subject my emotions to honour him that in everything I obey him." Do you agree with this statement? Explain.

8.

EXCURSUS:

"PRAISE AND WORSHIP"

—REV. DR. GARNETT ROPER

Away with your noisy hymns of praise! I will not listen to the music of your harps. [Amos 5:23-24]

I often try to get to worship services late in order to avoid the praise and worship session. But every now and then I am present when the praise and worship session is in full swing. I am clear that I have nothing against praise and I have nothing against worship. What I am against is an idiom that has spilled over from the mega church movementand has now come to be an indispensable part of worship services.

This session usually occupies about a quarter of the time allotted for a worship service. It involves multiple microphones and generally women and a splattering of men on the platform usually well dressed and singing a variety of imported songs. These songs usually follow the Gospel Ballard genre and are typically romantic both in tone and theme. It is more reliant on Old Testament rather than New Testament themes, language and understanding. In general the lyrical content uses words that have to do with worship, adoration, lifting up, praise, and the like. It hardly ever speaks of service, or helping and the worshipper is powerless to take action. The themes never speak of sin, but speak of forgiveness, and have a limited concept of struggle or suffering. Solutions are always instant and miraculous, individualized rather than corporate and collective.

I make the following criticisms and invite both challenge and discussion: the first is that praise and worship sessions lack artistic imagination. Choruses when they were first introduced in the public worship sessions were meant to give expression to the creativity of the worshipper reflecting upon their lived experience with God, share their story in testimony and song. The praise and worship sessions are sing over sessions. Very little emphasis is placed on improvisation. In fact there is an insipid uniformity to the sessions from church to church and from week to week.

The second criticism is that the songs do not reflect the lived experience of the people who are worshipping. There is a broader criticism to be made of much of the Caribbean experience of worship: the liturgy, prayer book, song books and sometimes the sermons are imported without the necessary changes having been made to give it a local accent. It is quite like those who wear their new suits with the tag in place so that it can be seen to be new and from elsewhere. The praise and worship songs are bad because they are artificially imposed on the experience of the people by the cultural penetration of the North Atlantic. What is worse is that it is imported from the same place all the time. There is a church creative and alive in Africa and the Asian sub-continent, but their music does not make into our church.

Thirdly, the praise and worship sessions alienate older members of the church. This is not to say that older members do not participate in the Praise and worship session—they do, and they sometimes like the songs. However, they are not the songs that they are used to singing. They are other people's new songs while their old songs have been left in the archives. More particularly, the songs do not represent the layering of experience which comes from the long years of struggle in the Christian pilgrimage. They do not resonate because they are not grappling with sin or suffering in a painstaking way. They are glib and frothy without being deep and engaging. They do not help the pastor to communicate the deep things of God at the bedside of some saint racked with pain and absurdity of human suffering. They are trite, clichéd and oversimplified.

Fourthly, the accent is on performance rather than participation. Worship is nothing if it is not participation. The songs are often chosen for the musicality of the song rather than the lyrical content. It is how the group sounds and whether they get to use the range of their voices more than whether or not some saint who has gone up the rough side of the mountain can recognize their situation in the song and be helped to carry on, that decides which song is chosen. It is much like a concert, from time to time the audience joins in. It is not however about them, it is about the stars on the stage/platform. The image cultivated by the present set of praise and worshippers could not make it past the dress and makeup rules of a generation ago. I have no time for those rules, but neither do I have time for the personal indulgence and vanity of the current crop of avant-garde dressers.

Fifthly, and this is perhaps the most important criticism, is that the songs have a right-wing ideology at their base. Every song sung encourages greater consumption. It encourages the imagination of enjoying more and more of this world's goods. It is capitalism at prayer. Many of these songs are written in the idiom of consumer advertising. They have been sanitized and used to speak about God's blessing, but one is not always sure if the accent is on God or it is on the blessings. Matthew's warning holds true, you cannot serve God and Mammon. The ideological content also includes the fact that some themes are ignored. How does modern worship help us to confront hunger or the experience of oppression or nakedness or homelessness? Is the individualization and privatization of the gospel not also the domestication of the gospel? Does this accent on light entertainment without reflecting on the existential urgency with which people are required to respond to their reality not make people more docile, gullible and powerless? How are people helped to appropriate the grace and power of God for their lived experience?

The gravamen of my argument is that we have a legacy in the Caribbean church in which our people when they had been emancipated first gain ownership and control over their bodies. They used their bodies in dance and their voice in song to critique and protest the society that was short-shrifting them and to imagine a better society for themselves. Building upon the legacy of resilience and resistance they have given to the world art forms that have been vehicles of the message of hope and the cry for justice. The question is can those same people with their imagination, passion and immense capacity for the arts give to God in worship, songs that are worth singing?

DISCUSSION QUESTIONS

1. Garnett Roper offers five points of critique about the Church's praise and worship today. Which did you find most difficult to accept? Explain.

2. How might we address the matter that we do not generally sing songs that mirror our experiences in good, artistic imagination?

3. What might the Church do to increase the participation of all congregants in praise and worship? Specifically, how might it increase the participation of males?

4. Many of our praise and worship songs are indeed inward focussed with an overt celebration of personal blessing. Can this really lead us into a "right-winged" and "capitalistic" way of thinking that bows to "materialism" as Roper states? Explain.

5. Reflect on the poem, "Come," that appears in the introduction to Section 2. While the people find it difficult to accept the Church's relevance to their daily lives, Jesus

nevertheless calls them to himself. Does the Church run the risk of pushing away would be inquirers? If it does how will these persons find accepting Christ's message possible?

PART 3:
Caring Again

LOOK, LISTEN, TEK IT IN, PUSH IT OUT

Di Bobo-dread tek 'im son
An' trod di road, di two a dem as man,
Broom pon dem 'ead, dem nah run,
Dem long dread unda dem tam.

"Why do you take your child
And keep him from learning in school?
It's no wonder that he will get wild
And will only respond to police rule."

'im look pon di 'oman an' seh,
Guidance mi sista, nuff respect due.
Mi affi raise an' grow 'im ina fimi way,
Since mi nuh wah him tun like you."

Offended di sister screwed up her face,
Looking at the Bobo she started to go red:
"Move from here, you are a disgrace,
Get from my presence with your dirty head!
My son will surely prosper,
From the learning of the best books,
He will sit at the feet of the best teachers,
Instead of following those like you crooks!"
The dreadlocks smiled and revealed

One tooth in an otherwise toothless gum,
He rocked back and on his brooms leaned
And shared some wise words and some.

"Sista yu nuh seem fi realize
Dat you yout' firs' learn from di way you ac'.
No 'mount a book aggo mek 'im actualize
An' show mannas, an' tell people t'anks.
Yu nuh seem fi memba
Dat when di fus' time yu see mi face
Yu neva even tek time fi bodda,
An' tell mi "mawning;" what a disgrace.

"Yout' an yout' learn more,
From how dem si dem people move bout
Dem look, den listen an' ebryting tek in,
An' wha dem si a dat dem push out.
Mek my yout walk bout wid me
Mek mi lead 'im ina my way.
At least 'im wi learn howdy ad tenk ye,
Because mi nuh want him like you be.

As the Church seeks to recapture its Biblical vision of the Kingdom of God it will come to understand that its platform pronouncements must be lived out in the community, especially in small ways that will have the most lasting impact on the future. When we focus on grand changes that will draw the greatest attention to our efforts we often miss the power of the sustained, behind the scenes involvement in people's lives that make the most profound impact on them. When we unashamedly pour Godly values of love and care in the lives of those with whom we come into contact, our message will help renew our nation through recapturing the gentleness, care and civility, which once characterized us. We dare not miss out on these little things, as in the scheme of things they are the neglected foxes that all too easily spoil our vines (Song of Solomon 2:15).

9.

TRUTH, BELIEFS, AND VALUES

Fix your thoughts on what is true, and honorable, and right, and pure, and lovely, and admirable. Think about things that are excellent and worthy of praise. [Philippians 4:8]

Our country has in the past few years been gripped in a raging debate about the place of truth, beliefs, and values in our daily lives. On the one hand, we have "progressives" who see these ideas as human creations, which have limited shelf-lives and ought to be dispensed with. On the other hand, "religious conservatives," who often paint themselves as the protectors of these essentials, fight a relentless war for their preservation. Here are five facts about truth, beliefs, and values that I believe ought to be considered, though I think the implications of each are so difficult that they might be deemed too inconvenient for us.

1. WE ALL BELIEVE IN ABSOLUTE TRUTH

The last half of the twentieth century signaled a significant change in the way the Western world viewed truth. The reality and horrors of wars, led by those espousing truth, led to various persons challenging popular concepts of right and wrong. When coupled with the age of technology and its greater access to knowledge, and as our world has shrunk making the other man's culture that much more knowable, the idea of absolute truth is brought into question. Are not our ideas of truth truly limited by our experiences, cultures, and contexts? If so (and yes it is so, experts say) whose absolute truth is more absolute?

That last question itself shows that there is no absolute truth. But here is the challenge: the statement that says, "There is no absolute truth," is itself a claim of absolute truth. For my statement to make sense that "there is no absolute truth," it does so by making an absolute statement. This philosophical conundrum has a very practical side to it—we cannot live as though there is no absolute truth since we would then have to say that no idea of truth is incorrect. Try living in a world like that. The really difficult question is, however, whose idea of absolute truth is at least "more absolute?" That question itself is a concern for another time and place.

2. WE ALL HAVE FAITH IN SOMETHING

The age of reason (modernism) has presented the idea that "belief" is bad. It exists only where there is a lack of knowledge, and so we ought to believe only until we know. The idea is that everything is knowable, even if we do not now know everything. Through the scientific method, we ought to suspend dependence on all beliefs, replacing such with the pursuit of knowledge. Those who insist on living by belief, usually religious or superstitious people, have little to offer to this world where scientific inquiry is to be prized. But let's examine that last claim for a moment—which scientific inquiry demonstrates that the ONLY way of knowing is through science?

There is no such scientific evidence, which means that the statement that we only know through science is itself a "belief." Belief is a part of the finite human condition. We are trying to make sense of this world that we cannot fully understand, and in spite of our best efforts, we have to begin the process of knowing with assumptions (beliefs). It is true that as we pursue knowledge we will find that we must shelve some of our beliefs. But there is no indication that we can be totally disdainful of all belief since some of them are foundational to human survival without a hint of scientific evidence—

for example, that murder is wrong, or that all things being equal, a deceptive person will be untrustworthy. This suggests, then, that "faith" is the starting point of all our knowledge. This might not be "religious faith" in the limited sense, but faith nonetheless, perhaps that a process of inquiry will lead to greater understanding, or the universe is of such that it will co-operate with our proper inquiry to yield "trustworthy truth." Of course, there is a more difficult question—whose and which faith and beliefs are "more acceptable?" Again, that is another question for another time and place.

3. WE ALL HAVE VALUES

The basic meaning of "values" is a set of beliefs or principles which we hold dear for life. Many times these beliefs and principles are passed on by religion, but more often they are passed on by family and culture, even for those who do not have a religious affiliation. When we insist that we should "be kind," or that "we should not lie," we are often declaring those things that we value—the importance of community and truth in these cases.

The insistence on values has gotten a bad rap in recent times, usually because religious persons are chided for trying to impose their "parochial values" on others. "Let us stop insisting on values and instead work for 'rights!'" Such is a popular cry that misses the point that all "rights" are first based on our values (as are all laws). The more important question is, "What is the motivation of our values, and which values are most important?"

4. WE ARE ALL PAROCHIAL TO OUR VALUES

The word "parochial" means "narrow and limited." By itself, it has no value judgment to it, but it has developed a pejorative meaning based on the way it has been used in today's world. People who are classed as parochial are cursed for their "narrow-mindedness," which is the hallmark of backwardness and lack of progress. Unfortunately, for anyone to maintain his/her values s/he has to be parochial to them. We often work in spaces where the dominant culture does not support our most cherished values. We may find, for instance, that it is offensive to be in a particular environment, but as long as we are there we do our best to maintain our "narrow and limited" way of thinking on an issue without running afoul of the more dominant culture. So a particular corporate culture sees customers as "dollar signs" and treats them that way. Everything it does is about preserving the bottom line, and as such its decisions are guided solely by profits. The person who values people more than money will remain "narrow and limited" on the matter, as long as that remains a part of his or her values. A more difficult question has to do with which values we ought to be parochial to and which we can dispense with? There is no easy answer.

5. WE ALL IMPOSE OUR VALUES ON OTHERS

There are times when we do not impose our values on others, but such is guarded by more important values. For instance, in the corporate culture we often abhor some of the values imposed from the top, but we yield to them because we value keeping our jobs as being more important than protesting, at least for the time. Now, if we think that management is wrong in imposing its values on others, just wait until we have a sense of control on what happens in our sphere of influence—we then impose our values on others. We do it with our children; our classrooms operate by them; they set the tone of our offices. We cannot help but impose them. I heard a statement once that Dancehall artist, Vybz Kartel, famous for some of the raunchiest and most sexually-explicit songs recorded in recent times, insists that his children do not listen to those songs. Vybz himself has publicly said that church and religious people ought to realize that they should not impose their beliefs and values on others, while he does so with his own family.

We also expect our government to impose a new set of values on our people, in keeping with trends that will advance us economically. There is just no way in our modern world that those in control ought not to be expected to do this. But in all of this, the greater question is, "Which are the values that we can more legitimately impose?"

MOVING FORWARD

I think an open and honest discussion needs to be had on these matters. As we fight our "culture wars," insistence without admission of the difficulties that exist on all sides of these issues only leads to greater division and destruction of us as a people. We paint unsavoury pictures of those with whom we disagree, and we twist facts and ideas to support our points. Finger pointing, name calling, and character assassination become the order of the day. I have some practical suggestions for the church as we face difficult issues that challenge our traditional values and morality.

First, we need to make it known that there is no shame in listening to the voices that differ from ours while holding to our positions. I trust that we can properly defend the value of our beliefs and values since they are rooted in truth. If they are truthful then there is nothing to fear from those who differ from us. Maybe it is that we refrain from engaging them because of the influence they might have on the gullible. But they will influence the gullible, whether inside or outside of the church. Additionally, if we deliberately engage those who differ from us we might give them the opportunity, in a non-threatening environment, to better understand our concerns and perhaps even adopt them as theirs. If the truth causes us to change our beliefs in line with our detractors, there is still no shame in that.

Second, and building on the first, we ought to create actual opportunities where detractors can meet us in discussions on these issues. Could you imagine what it would be like if a church, known for its rejection of homosexuality as a viable option for our society, engaged in a discussion on the needs of the gay-community in today's Jamaica? I suspect that in-between the polar opposite of positions on the issue between the Church and its critics are a continuum of issues, many of which the church could readily attempt to address. In fact, such openness to discussion would put the church in touch with a constituency with which it normally has limited contact. If the church believes that homosexuals can be counselled out of the practice, it presents such persons with the best opportunity to get the necessary help when it engages them in respectful discussion.

Finally, for the purposes of this publication, the church has got to be prepared to constantly ward off detractors from inside and outside. Truth and its implications cannot be bought, and those who would defend truth must know that it has a penchant for squeezing those who find it inconvenient. There is much more value in losing the support of those who disagree with us than changing our values to accommodate detractors. Truth that easily changes, and the beliefs and values that ensue from them, perhaps are not worth keeping.

DISCUSSION QUESTIONS

1. Are the concerns of this chapter worth considering? Explain.

2. In light of what we have read in the chapter how might we respond to the claim that we should readily release our values when dealing with others?

3. There is no guarantee that in living out our values, in spite of our best efforts, others will not be offended by them. How should we address this fact?

4. Is it really practical to give a listening ear to those with whom we differ? Explain. What do you make of the suggestion that the Church ought not to be afraid to engage members of the gay community if we truly believe our values are based on the truth? What practical steps might we have to take to make such a forum happen?

5. "There is much more value in losing the support of those who disagree with us than changing our values to accommodate detractors. Truth that easily changes, and

the beliefs and values that ensue from them, perhaps are not worth keeping." Is there a danger in such a position? How might we minimize such a danger?

10.

THAT BLASTED WOMAN!

If you are faithful in little things, you will be faithful in large ones. But if you are dishonest in little things, you won't be honest with greater responsibilities. [Luke 16:10]

I am certain to get myself in trouble for the reflection in this chapter. I read Delano Franklyn's ideas on the failure of Ponzi schemes in Jamaica (Observer April 25, 2010), where he lays the blame squarely at the feet of the lack of ethical dealings by us as Jamaicans. Franklyn laments the fact that we want what's due to us from others but do our best (and worse) to get what is not our due, as long as we can get away with it. In other words, we assiduously look out for our best interest even if that means that we are totally inconsiderate of others. Franklyn believes that this must be reversed if we are to see improvement in our stocks as Jamaicans. I totally agree with him, and ardently contend that though we have economic challenges as a nation, it is our ethics and morality that have left us in the ditch we have fallen in. It is also one of the central concerns of the message of Christianity, which we often ignore.

Now the trouble: though we see what Franklyn is speaking about in our attempt to cheat the Jamaica Public Service, the Tax-man, and the National Water Commission, our inconsideration is also seen in our oblivious behaviour to others, for instance, when standing in a line to do some business. And here I have some questions, wishing indeed that there would be some logical (even scientific) answers, if possible. Why is it that women change their minds so often about what it is they need while standing at the cashier at the store? And why do they wait until they get their bills from the cashier before beginning the almighty search for the money in their bags? My son and I stood a full seven or eight minutes behind a woman in a Burger King restaurant in Kingston while she and her teenage daughter sought to buy two sandwiches. It did not help that there was one cashier working. I wish this were an uncommon occurrence, but in my experience, it is not. And each time I experience it I hear my dearly departed mom and my alive dad (yes, both) speaking to me from my first days negotiating my way in shops and stores with them: "Hi, people are behind you waiting! Hurry up! You know how much the thing cost, so you must have your money ready!"

Can someone tell me why is it that more women struggle with this than men do? Do not get me wrong; I have seen more men than women attempting to break lines, for instance, without a concern for the 100 behind them. In fact, I have hardly seen women with this particular indiscretion until recently at camp, where a group of young women refused to join lines for meals, attempting to cut in at the front, while all the males dutifully joined the lines. Generally, though, why do men break lines more than women do, without a care for others in them? These are just small manifestations of a bigger concern.

It seems to me that the idea that "he who is faithful in small things will be rewarded with big things" is at work here. The point is that small victories prepare us for bigger ones. But the converse is also true—failure in small things is a portent of bigger failures to come. And the small matter of being considerate of others seems to be the very basis of so many bigger ethical dealings in life. Just think about it; if I really do not care about you I will find it easier to take for myself what belongs to you. It may begin with taking your space in the line or taking my inordinate time while you wait, but that is really just a small step from me taking your money, and God forbid your life. My wife and I had an experience in Florida some years ago when she inadvertently left her handbag in a Wal-Mart store. When we went back to get it, some good Samaritan had found it and dutifully turned it at the lost-and-found... and left $30 in the bag, taking only $170 (so kind of him/her). What does that person teach his/her kids about stealing? Usually, a dialogue between parent and child in such circumstances in our country goes something like this:

CHILD: *"Dad, is stealing wrong?"*

FATHER: (While taking the money from the bag) *"Of course it is! And don't let me ever hear of you taking what does not belong to you! Do you hear me! It is not good to be a t'ief?*

CHILD: (If the JPS ad is to be believed) *"Then, how come you taking the woman money from her bag? How come?"*

FATHER: *Pickney, don't ask me no feisty question! You a work an' earn money? Bright! These pickneys of today, you see! A which part dem come from, eeh? Always a gi big people nuff lip!*

If the adage is correct that children live what they learn, then such behaviour will only perpetuate itself. I wonder if anyone has done a survey to see how many persons would think that they ought to return the bag with everything in it. Maybe one of you could do such a survey, even informally, and share the results with us.

I hear the words of a wise man resounding in my mind. We must adopt them as guiding life principles if we are going to see improvements in our stocks as a nation:

Don't push your way to the front; don't sweet-talk your way to the top. Put yourself aside, and help others get ahead. Don't be obsessed with getting your own advantage. Forget yourselves long enough to lend a helping hand.

Whether we are man or woman, boy or girl, we have to catch this spirit for the sake of our country. We cannot continue to live as though our greatest goal is to "feather our own caps" even if that is at the expense of others. And this is a message that we must push at all levels of society and in each family. It is definitely a message that is central to the faith most of us profess. It then must become more central to what we say to others and how we live and must be of foremost importance to the teaching of the Church.

DISCUSSION QUESTIONS

1. Do you agree with Delano Franklyn's idea that we have a penchant for seeking what we do not deserve, even if it comes at the expense of others? Explain.

2. The Jamaican person is often chided for his "anancyism" in dealing with others as a means of material gain at the expense of others. Are there social factors that have "bred" that in us, if you think it is true?

3. What do you make of the writer's assessment that our failure to do right in the small things is a gateway to bigger failures in our lives?

4. The writer makes a connection between our people's failure to do the right thing and the practice in children? Is this an inevitable process? How might we address it even if the parents in our community do not change?

5. "We cannot continue to live as though our greatest goal is to 'feather our own caps' even if that is at the expense of others. And this is a message that we must push

at all levels of society and in each family. It is definitely a message that is central to the faith most of us profess." Do you agree with this assessment? Explain. How might the Church address this reality?

11.

MOLDING CARING CHILDREN

Fathers,do not provoke your children to anger by the way you treat them. Rather, bring them up with the discipline and instruction that comes from the Lord. [Ephesians 6:4]

Recently, instead of marking my papers as a good theological lecturer should, I searched YouTube for my favourite cartoon of all time. In the 1970s, for a short time on our sole TV station at the time, JBC, "Milton the Monster" graced our screens one evening per week. I loved the show, perhaps because of its absolutely fabulous theme song and the fact that the show chronicled the hilarious tale of a monster, who because of a blunder of his maker, turned out so...sweet. I was so happy to find Milton on You-Tube and passed a bit of time watching and laughing again. I have not regretted putting those boring papers aside.

As I listened to the theme song again the tremendous truth of the lyrics suddenly hit me like the proverbial ton of bricks. There in the song lies a profound line that the world needs to latch on to, especially for those of us in strife-torn Jamaica. For those of you who neither remember the cartoon nor the lyrics of the theme song, I display the latter below (check YouTube for the show itself. It is well worth the time). The song recounts the creation of Milton the Monster by Professor Weirdo and his mad assistant, Count Kook. The Professor is making Milton via a boiling potion that has been thrown into cast shaped something like Frankenstein:

PROFESSOR WEIRDO: *"Six drops of yessence of terror; five drops of sinister sauce."*

COUNT KOOK: *"When the stirring's done may I lick the spoon?"*

PROFESSOR WEIRDO: *"Of course, ha, ha, of course! Now for the tincture of-a tenderness, but I must use only a touch, for, without a touch of tenderness, it might destroy me... oops too much! (Count Kook accidentally hits the hand of the Professor as he is throwing his tincture of tenderness in the mixture; almost the entire flask is poured in). Better hold your breath it's starting to tick."*

COUNT KOOK: *"Better hold my hand I'm feeling sick!"*

MILTON (now alive): *"Hello, Daddy!"*

PROFESSOR WEIRDO: *"What have I done?"*
MILTON: *I'm Milton, your brand new son."*

The whole point of the cartoon is that the Professor has failed in his attempt to create a real evil monster by putting too much tenderness in the mixture. Milton goes about the place doing good deeds, giving flowers to people, and looking out for those whom he perceives as needy. The professor despises his "un-monsterly" conduct and is doing his best to get rid of Milton, week after week. But all fail, and Milton remains a loyal, unsuspecting (almost naïve) model son.

Is this not the reality of Jamaica in reverse? Think for a moment of the link between tenderness shown to children and the resulting gentle, caring adults that they then develop into, as suggested in theory. Anecdotally, too many Jamaican children grow up without tenderness. Usually, overstressed single mothers struggle to eke out a living in a society that provides little real opportunities for appropriate education and employment. Children are often left unattended or in the care of other children who cannot offer the assistance necessary for their proper development. From early they learn that they have to fend for themselves, often against those who do not have their best interest at heart, or who do not show this to them. Add to this the fact that many of our communities (200 according to the government) are so ravaged by poverty and violence that it is a common belief that the "tender touch" approach is not appropriate to help children navigate the uncaring world that they will grow up to see. It seems as if, though we have not meant to create monsters, we have been more successful than Professor Weirdo in accomplishing the task many times over. We have not put any tenderness in the mix and now we are being destroyed by the resulting creation.

There are so many points to consider in effectively finding a solution to the problem of Jamaica's growing population of vile monsters, but here, I want to mention just one—how we live with our children to make them the gentle giants our society requires. The harsh treatment of children is neither limited to Jamaica nor to our present day. Society has always struggled with the reality of child abuse, and apparently the most vocal against the practice were (surprise, surprise) major religious leaders. Even then, not all religions have strong teachings against child abuse, but Judaism, Christianity, and Islam do.

The famous Shema passage of Deuteronomy forms the basis of child-rearing practices among Jews. The Shema is rooted in the idea that parents, in their love for God, ought to live in ways that will encourage their children to embrace

His teachings. Though other portions encourage the use of corporal punishment with children (e.g. Proverbs 29:15), it is the life of example that the Jewish scriptures hold up as the supreme responsibility of parents:

Attention, Israel! God, our God! God the one and only! Love God, your God, with your whole heart: love him with all that's in you, love him with all you've got! Write these commandments that I've given you today on your hearts. Get them inside of you and then get them inside your children. Talk about them wherever you are, sitting at home or walking in the street; talk about them from the time you get up in the morning to when you fall into bed at night. Tie them on your hands and foreheads as a reminder; inscribe them on the doorposts of your homes and on your city gates. [Deuteronomy 6:4-9—The Message]

By the time of Jesus, however, we see where popular culture had come to view children as an imposition, or at least a distraction to serious things. Jesus, understanding the Shema, had a different approach:

One day children were brought to Jesus in the hope that he would lay hands on them and pray over them. The disciples shooed them off. But Jesus intervened: "Let the children alone, don't prevent them from coming to me. God's kingdom is made up of people like these." After laying hands on them, he left. [Matthew 19;13-15, the Message]

No doubt this formed the basis for Paul's understanding of the issue of raising children. Listen to his explanation of how he lived among the Thessalonians and then his warning to parents in Ephesus:

With each of you we were like a father with his child, holding your hand, whispering encouragement, showing you step-by-step how to live well before God, who called us into his own kingdom, into this delightful life. [1 Thessalonians 2:11-12—The Message]

Fathers, don't exasperate your children by coming down hard on them. Take them by the hand and lead them in the way of the Master. [Ephesians 6:4—The Message]

The most often quoted passage from the Bible about child rearing in Jamaica, and which is often used to justify harsh corporal punishment, is interestingly not in the Bible as quoted by many ("Spare the rod and spoil the child"). It is more of a common-sense application of Proverbs 13:24, which tells us that, "He that spareth his rod hateth his son: but he that loveth him chasteneth him betimes (KJV)." Perhaps it is that last word that has us confused into accepting a distorted understanding of the text. The word "betimes" is better translated "diligently" in other translations. But what does it mean to use the rod diligently? The Hebrew word so translated has the connotation of "early", or "before it is too late." Thus, the emphasis of the passage is not on constant and intense discipline, but on timely discipline in the formative years of the child as a means of guiding him in the right path.

Too many Jamaican families practice harsh discipline in children, even when the child has passed the age when such discipline is useful. I recall seeing a mother viciously beat her sixteen-year-old daughter who returned from school at 5:00 pm, instead of the designated 4:00. This was done openly in a tenement yard setting, where my mechanic had his car shop, in full view of all in the yard. For that mother, her daughter was showing signs of disobedience that should be driven out since no one should be able to say that her daughter's waywardness was due to a mother's failure to discipline her.

And, according to my mechanic, this was a regular occurrence, which obviously was not working. He and his wife had their four well-disciplined children constantly around them, ages ranged from 4 to 18, and never was a harsh word or action used against them, at least not in the sight of others. Whatever discipline he and his wife used worked well, and all his children have grown to be very respectful and diligent in whatever they do. What the Bible teaches and how we use it to justify our actions is often at odds with each other.

Islam also has a greater affinity to the attitude of the Shema, at least in the teachings of the Hadith, than with the frequently reported abuse of children in many Islamic nations. The Hadith (pl.) form the second most important writings among Muslims, and relate the teachings and practices of the Prophet of Allah (peace be upon him), which Muslims are mandated to follow:

The Prophet of Allah (peace be upon him) kissed Hasan ibn 'Ali (his grandson) while Aqra' ibn Habis was sitting nearby. Aqra' said, "I have ten children and have never kissed one of them.' The Prophet (peace be upon him) looked at him and said, 'Those who show no mercy will be shown no mercy."[Bukhari, Volume No. 91]

To this day, in many traditional Islamic communities, the discipline of boys includes the guidance of a male teacher, who instructs groups of boys in what it means to be responsible men in the community. Boys often sit quietly in rows and listen to the instruction, rooted in the Qu'ran and Hadith and slanted to practical issues of the day. In most cases, those boys have no choice but to attend these sessions since they are sent there by fathers themselves who require it of them and see to it that they attend. Spanking may be used in these families, but those faithful in the teaching of the religious texts understand that it is but one practice among many, which are used for the formation of the youth.

The abuse of our religious teachings by many has led others to disregard them altogether. What has ensued is a generation of youngsters who have not been brought up with an understanding of boundaries or personal responsibilities. In our attempts to be our children's friends we have forgotten discipline in a timely way and it is almost as if we have poured indiscipline in their lives instead. Perhaps Professor Weirdo would have been more successful in creating a monster of his liking by just altogether neglecting to discipline Milton. A lack of discipline is indeed not the same as not showing tenderness, but both the "no-tenderness" and "no-discipline" approaches end up creating seriously dysfunctional children.

The wisdom of these religions seems to confirm Professor Weirdo's concern—more than a touch of tenderness will lead to tender, caring children. But the new-found distrust of religion and its ensuing lack of discipline also destroy our children and then our society. Who will lead the charge to change this? Could our churches lead the charge in addressing this imbalance? I recommend that our churches spearhead what I call, "Family Institutes," where through research, parenting seminars, mentoring programmes, homework clubs, marital counseling, etc., we take on the mandate of re-socializing our families through a disciplined and reasonable tenderness. Our society requires it; are our churches up to it?

DISCUSSION QUESTIONS

1. Is the lack of tenderness in our child-rearing practices as big a deal as the writer asserts? Explain.

2. News of the abuse of children by their parents or guardians has become more prevalent today? Do you think there is really an increase in child abuse, or are the stories becoming better known? What rationale do you have for your answer?

3. As with many other things in our community, the Bible is often used to justify the abuse of our children. Should this be of concern to the Church? Explain.

4. While there is the evidence of physical and emotional abuse of our children there are increasing allegations of parents failing to instil discipline in their offspring? Do you agree with the writer that both practices "create seriously dysfunctional children?" Explain.

5. "I recommend that our churches spearhead what I call, "Family Institutes," where

through research, parenting seminars, mentoring programmes, homework clubs, marital counseling, etc., we take on the mandate of re-socializing our families through a disciplined and reasonable tenderness." What are your thoughts on this suggestion?

12.

CLEANING UP AFTER EACH OTHER

But among you it will be different. Whoever wants to be a leader among you must be your servant, and whoever wants to be first among you must become your slave." [Matthew 20:26-27]

I was annoyed when I once again saw dishes in the sink. My teenaged sons have to be hounded to do their duties, and once my wife or I go off to bed with the chore not yet completed we can be assured that someone will forget his duty, or was too busy doing something else to get to it. It has been a recurring theme in my house, and no strategy we have tried to address the problem (and we have tried many) has succeeded. Cleaning up after each other does not come easily to my boys, and in speaking to the parents of their friends the trait is much more common than we might think. In my home, I have found that it is much easier for me to do the dishes as soon as I use them, and it seems to me that if we all just did that then there would be no pile-up and we'd all be responsible for only a few. My wife thinks that such an approach does not teach the value of caring for each other and contributing to the wellbeing of all. But the problem has persisted for years now and the quarrels that ensue have weighed heavily on me.

I cannot say that I grew-up doing household chores. I grew up a city boy, the youngest of four boys for many years until a sister and another brother came along. In those days it was not common for city boys to have chores, for two reasons: household chores were the responsibility of girls and, in a case like ours with a house full of boys and two working parents, there was a household helper employed for cooking and cleaning. Our family was never rich; in fact, we were at best lower middle-class. But we always had a helper because it was inconceivable in those days for a city home with our dynamics to be any different. So the helper did the chores during the week and Mom did them on weekends. After my sister came along and could do so, she shared in some of those responsibilities.

In 1974 my parents went away for four weeks to England. My father was sent on a business trip and the company for which he worked allowed my mother to accompany him, all expenses paid. In those four weeks my Grand Aunt, Aunt Horty, came to stay with us. But at 74 she could not do it all, and since we at the time needed a new household helper my parents hired Rema Dempster, who was at that time in her mid-20s. She became the longest-serving helper my family ever had, and her family (four children and a husband) became like our family. I still speak of Ms. Rema as my second mother and still have fond conversations with members of her family when we see each other.

The relationship between my mother and Ms. Rema was one of profound mutual respect. I cannot remember ever hearing my mother speak an ill-word about her, nor do I remember her speaking one of my mother. In any case, Mummy had always drilled it in us not to disrespect our helpers, as they too were people working for the benefit of their families. This principle might have been doubly enforced with Ms. Rema, and in hindsight, my experience with her has profoundly impacted my view of "chores" and those who do "menial" tasks.

More than anything else, however, it was the going off to college and then moving from the family home that forced me to begin the "chore" regime. I had to prepare my own meals, clean my own house and even wash my clothes. Much of this came full force when I moved to Central Jamaica for work and lived by myself in a rural town without a laundromat; additionally, I did not earn enough to be able to afford a helper or to constantly eat from restaurants. In the main, I had to do all for myself and steadily improved at all of them over the years.

Significantly, also, was a growing understanding from my theological studies that a life of service was closest to the example of Christ, and I came not only to appreciate my domestic chores but, confirming what I had imbibed from the experience with Ms. Rema, I developed an even more profound respect for those who make their living from it. These experiences have helped me form fairly strong attitudes towards how I function in my family and doing the tasks formerly done by helpers in my upbringing is seen as essential.

Today my family finds it financially impossible to afford a full-time helper, but we do have a "Day's Worker" who comes in one day a week to clean our apartment. Our attempts have always been to treat such persons as equals, and to pay them more than the minimum wage since we still do not know how anyone lives on such. It is not lost on me that this is not a normal way of thinking among most, as very few persons I know share my thoughts. And that apparently includes my sons (hopefully for the time being) who view the doing of dishes as a task a bit too difficult to enjoy or to do consistently.

Maybe it is that in Jamaica's fairly well-stratified existence, we have been conditioned to see manual labour as the duties of those at the very bottom of society. There is still a high priority placed on jobs requiring "book learning," though in recent years we see that changing. So many still clamour to be doctors, lawyers, engineers, and accountants, seeing such as their passport to an existence free of the shackles of manual labour. With way less than ten percent (10%) of Jamaica's population attaining tertiary education, the vast majority of our people will work in jobs at the lower levels of organizations, and many will be at the very bottom if they are lucky enough to have a job.

What then do most of our people do for earning a living? Apart from the thousands who have no jobs and have mastered the arts of hustling and begging, quite a few function as household helpers, gardeners, gas station attendants, servers in fast food restaurants and corner-shops, and a growing number are becoming security guards. Many are industrious miracle workers, managing to care for their families, feeding, clothing, and schooling three or four children with their limited resources. And many of these families lack the participation, care, and support of a husband and father who shares in the struggle. Jamaica was built on the backs of a marginalized majority, and today it continues to be sustained in the same way.

It is then interesting to me that so many of us in the church hold to views that continue to treat our people with little regard. Of course, you will never hear a disparaging word about our hard-working people uttered from our platforms. I suspect that the Pastor who would be brave enough to castigate the bulk of the congregation for their low status in society will soon find the church coffers depleted since these are the masses whose "likkle tups" here and there add up to meet the largest share of the budget of the church. But there is a growing sense of division in our churches, built on the deliberate attempt of our leaders to distance themselves "from the bottom."

Never before have we had so many titled pastors among us; our congregations are led by Doctors, Bishops, Super Apostles, Prophets, and many other superiorly titled ones, who through some divine favour have attained new heights in a flash, setting them apart from the rest. Unfortunately, with this comes the understanding that particular tasks are beneath their status, and it is the little woman again who is left pushing the broom and cleaning up after the others.

The above reality hit me some years ago when I was attending a conference of theological college administrators, which drew many attendants from across the Caribbean and North America. One of the plenary sessions was on incorporating "Servant Leadership" in the day-to-day running of our theological institutions. As the session entered its discussion phase, much unease became evident, as the administrators grappled with the reality that in the practice of their duties they had largely ignored Jesus' call that the greatest among us must serve the least (Matthew 23:11).

As is the case when dis-ease is evident, silence ensues but then becomes too much of a burden for the people to bear. One administrator spoke up to defend himself why he did not practice servanthood in his ministries. He was a District Overseer, the President of his denomination's Bible school, the Pastor of one of the largest churches in the denomination, as well as a missionary, sent from overseas, all for which he was paid individually and handsomely. He said, "I really want to serve my people like Jesus did, but my daily duties make that impossible." At the same time his associate Pastor known personally to me, and who did the bulk of the administrative and daily pastoral work in the church was not earning enough to care for his small family.

No thought was given to his predicament because unlike his Pastor he had not yet been titled —he had not yet arrived, so the menial tasks were left to him.

We have to be careful then that we do not say to our people that the task of cleaning up after each other is left to them because they are at the bottom. The message of Christ is that we clean-up after each other—all of us. It is called "service" and finds its model in the example of Jesus, who did not see equality with God as holding on to entitlement, but instead saw it as serving others, even to the point of death (Philippians 2). It is a hard message and given our dastardly history of the marginalization which came with slavery and has remained entrenched, too many of us see serving others as a requirement of those who cannot do better.

Whether it is the washing up of dishes, or washing the sores of the poor, or caring for the old, grumpy sister who gets on our last nerve, we had better come to see that "cleaning up after each other" is the way of the Master, and any Christianity that is not built on that principle, expecting that of all (Lawyer, Doctor and Indian Chief included), is not the Christianity of the Bible. Well, that's how I see it.

DISCUSSION QUESTIONS

1. This chapter celebrates the privilege of serving others. Is serving really a privilege? Or is it just a responsibility? Explain.

2. The author suggests that our people's dislike of serving others might have come from our history of social stratification, where servanthood was expected of the lower classes and greeted with disdain by those on top? Do you agree?

3. Does Jamaican society still maintain the tradition of exempting boys from household chores? If so, is this really a problem? Explain.

4. How can our Churches be faithful to the message of Christ if our leaders do not insist on, and demonstrate obedient service to others (even the lowly)? Does our failure in emphasizing such an emphasis remove a necessary plank of Christianity? Explain.

5. What is the poem, *"Look, Listen, Tek it in, Push it out,"* in the introduction to Section

3 really about? How might the Church be guilty of some of the maladies suggested by the poem? How is your Church (if you are a Church goer) different? How can we ensure that we practice respect to each and every person in society?

About the Author

David Pearson is former Academic Dean at the Jamaica Theological Seminary, where he continues to lecture in Theology and the Humanities. He has been involved in Christian ministry for over thirty years. He is a graduate of the Jamaica Theological Seminary and the Caribbean Graduate School of Theology, and is a MPhil/PhD student at the United Theological College of the West Indies.

David is an ardent Bible Teacher and Bible Study Leader who has devoted much of his life to helping others understand the message of the Bible and how it might help in the transformation of their lives, families, and communities. His speciality is Inductive Bible Study with traditional Church audiences and Contextual Bible Study with marginalized peoples.

David is also involved in Community and Youth Development. He has worked as a Conflict Resolution trainer with PALS Jamaica, and is a Moral Educator with Family Life Tobago, an organization working in Secondary schools in Tobago to bring character education to teenagers and their families.

David has taught locally and internationally for many years. Apart from his various engagements in Jamaica, he has helped Church leaders and lay persons in Canada, Honduras, Haiti, Cuba, Tanzania, St. Lucia, St. Vincent, and Trinidad and Tobago.

He is passionate about assisting persons in seeing the relevance of the Bible to their transformation as people of character. He is married with two sons and heavily involved in his Church's community witness.

www.ingramcontent.com/pod-product-compliance
Lightning Source LLC
Chambersburg PA
CBHW060829050426
42453CB00008B/633